Life
on the American Frontier

Frontiersmen and their families were self-sufficient. Make-do governed not only their attitude toward tools and clothing, but their diet and their leisure time, little as that was. Life in the frontier towns, such as St. Louis, was sometimes less an adventure and sometimes more, since such towns were jumping-off points for the wilderness. It was a hard and primitive life for the homesteaders and the trappers, but it probably did not seem as hard to the American of that day as it does to us nowadays.

The Author

LOUIS B. WRIGHT was director of the Folger Shakespeare Library in Washington, D.C., for twenty years before retiring in 1968. As a member of the Permanent Research Group of the Huntington Library (1932–1948), Dr. Wright was primarily concerned with research in the field of the English Renaissance and American civilization of the colonial period. He is the author of scores of magazine articles, monographs, and books dealing with early times in America. Dr. Wright has been awarded more than twenty honorary degrees from universities here and abroad, and he is a member of various advisory boards in the arts and letters.

"Tomahawk and Sabre, or Even Chances." From a photograph of a painting by C. Schreyvogel. Courtesy, Library of Congress.

LIFE ON THE

AMERICAN FRONTIER

BY LOUIS B. WRIGHT

Capricorn Books

G. P. PUTNAM'S SONS, NEW YORK

LIFE IN  AMERICA

Edited by Louis B. Wright

Everyday Life In Colonial America
by Louis B. Wright

Everyday Life in Twentieth Century America
by John W. Dodds

Everyday Life in the Age of Enterprise
by Robert H. Walker

Everyday Life on the American Frontier
by Louis B. Wright

Capricorn Books Edition 1971

Copyright © 1968 by Louis B. Wright
Fifth Impression

All rights reserved. Published simultaneously in
the Dominion of Canada by Longmans Canada
Limited, Toronto.

Library of Congress Catalog Card
Number: 68-24556

SBN: 399-20048-7

PRINTED IN THE UNITED STATES OF AMERICA
12216

Contents

List of Illustrations

Preface

The present volume does not pretend to give a new interpretation of the American frontier or to present a body of new facts. It is intended to provide in a brief compass a description of some of the motivations that sent the American people ever westward in search of fortunes in the fur trade, in the mines, on ranches, and on farms. We have ever been a race of optimists, always believing that we would have better luck beyond the mountains, across the deserts, somewhere in a new country toward the western sun. Restlessness has been in our blood. That restlessness helps account for the filling up of the North American continent by people lured there from the older settled regions in the East and from most of the countries of Europe.

Few subjects have attracted more attention from historians, travelers, and writers of fiction than the westward movement. I am indebted to many books, but to none more than to Ray A. Billington's *Westward Expansion*. I have in a few instances cited other works to which I am especially indebted. Full bibliographies are provided in Billington for those who wish to read further in the story of life on the American frontier, whether it was in early Virginia or in late-nineteenth-century Nebraska.

A few years ago I published *Everyday Life in Colonial*

America, like other volumes in this series designed to appeal particularly to young people. It was reviewed in an English journal as a work for serious scholars, and my efforts to express myself in nonacademic terminology was treated as oversimplification for Englishmen. I trust that no comment in this volume will sound too simple for any reader in the Thames Valley who may find a brief sketch of westering Americans worth his eyesight.

Four members of the Folger Library staff have been of immense help in the preparation of this volume. Mrs. Elaine W. Fowler has assisted with the research, especially in the selection of pictures. Miss Virginia LaMar has read the manuscript with a critical eye. Mrs. Barbara Kemple has been unfailingly cheerful when asked to type the author's untidy copy and has helped with the index. And Miss Megan Lloyd has read the proof.

LOUIS B. WRIGHT

1

The First Frontiers

WHEN a European thinks of the word "frontier," he remembers the border between countries, the point at which inspectors examine his luggage and check his passport. Or, latterly, he may think of a grimmer line between antagonistic nations, a line marked by barbed wire, minefields, and a few checkpoints heavily guarded by machine guns. But for the American, the word "frontier" means something vastly different. It has for him a variety of connotations that appeal to his imagination. Nowadays it may recall to addicts of television the wagon trains, Indian attacks, and gunmen of the Wild West or feuds between cattlemen and farmers—that complex of story material relating to the settlement of the Western country beyond the line of Eastern civilization. To the historian, the word "frontier" means the moving line of settlements between established and organized society and the wilderness or desert beyond.

In 1893, Frederick Jackson Turner, one of the great historians of the past generations, read a paper at the annual meeting of the American Historical Association with the

13

title: "The Significance of the Frontier in American History." The point of departure for Turner's paper was the end of free land in the West that could be had merely by staking a claim and making rudimentary improvements on it. The vast "frontier" of free government land was closed, and Turner's paper was an analysis of the effect on the nation and its development exerted by regions of free land in the West—a West that was ever receding until it reached the Pacific Ocean—where adventurous or restless men and women could establish new homes and work out the patterns of civilization under which they would live. Turner's essay proved enormously influential on later writers, some of whom saw in frontier conditions factors that altered the shape of older patterns of conduct and even of government. Excessive emphasis on the influence of the frontier produced a reaction that has tended to modify the conclusions of the disciples of Turner. Nevertheless, everyone recognizes the importance of the ever-moving zone of frontier life, though the interpretations of the impact of that influence vary widely.

The first frontier of what became the United States in later times was the line beyond the thinly scattered settlements along the Atlantic seaboard from Jamestown to Plymouth. These early settlements, precariously clinging to the Atlantic shore on the edge of an illimitable and hostile wilderness, made up England's first frontier in the New World. The hard and primitive conditions of life in these settlements would be reenacted thousands of times in the next three centuries, albeit frontiersmen learned from experience to be less helpless than were the early settlers at Jamestown.

Students of colonial settlement have often wondered at the incapacity and ineptitude of the colonists who settled at Jamestown, particularly during the "starving time" in the winter of 1609–10. At hand was a river teeming with fish, and all around lay woods filled with deer and other game;

nevertheless, they nearly perished from hunger. But we might remember that most of the colonials were accustomed to town life; many were Londoners who knew no more about fishing and hunting than they could have acquired by hearsay. And all were terrified of the deep woods, where Indians lurked ready to brain the unwary with a tomahawk.

Nobody yet knew what crops would grow in the soil of Virginia, what the weather would be like during the four seasons, what wild fruits and plants were edible or what might be poisonous. The settlers were even handicapped when it came to building habitations for themselves. Though trees abounded, they had not yet learned to build the log cabin, the type of structure that characterized later frontiers. They knew how to make bricks and build brick houses but that was slow and tedious work. Some knew how to make mud and wattle huts like those used by poorer people in certain country districts of England, but these were not very durable or satisfactory. Gradually they learned to adapt new materials to their needs, to saw and hew timbers to make wooden houses. Much later, after the coming of Germans and Swedes, frontiersmen learned to build dwellings out of notched logs, pigpen style, and to chink the cracks with mud or plaster.

Later frontiersmen knew precisely what they wanted, how they proposed to exist, and what they hoped would be their ultimate means of livelihood. The first colonists were uncertain about their purposes. The earliest ones came as employees of a stock company which itself had only vague notions of how it would turn the colony to profit. Stories of the discovery of gold by the Spaniards died hard, and nearly all the first settlers dreamed of finding gold or silver mines. Instead of mining gold at Jamestown, the settlers dug sassafras roots and loaded returning ships with cargoes of this aromatic shrub, then believed to have unusual curative power and to be a sovereign remedy for many of the ills of mankind.

THE INCONVENIENCIES
THAT HAVE HAPPENED TO SOME PER-
SONS WHICH HAVE TRANSPORTED THEMSELVES

from *England* to *Virginia*, vvithout prouisions necessary to sustaine themselues, hath
greatly hindred the Progresse of that noble Plantation: For preuention of the like disorders
heereafter, that no man suffer, either through ignorance or misinformation; it is thought re-
quisite to publish this short declaration: wherein is contained a particular of such necessaries, as either priuate families or single persons shall haue cause to furnish themselues with, for their better
support at their first landing in *Virginia*; whereby also greater numbers may receiue in part,
directions how to prouide themselues.

	li.	s.	d.
Apparrell.			
One Monmouth Cap	∞	OI	IO
Three falling bands		OI	03
Three shirts		07	06
One waste-coate		02	
One suite of Canuase		07	06
One suite of Frize		IO	00
One suite of Cloth		15	00
Three paire of Irish stockins		04	
Foure paire of shooes		08	08
One paire of garters	∞	00	IO
One doozen of points		00	03
One paire of Canuase sheets		08	00
Seuen ells of Canuase, to make a bed and boulster, to be filled in *Virginia* 8.s.			
One Rug for a bed 8. s. which with the bed seruing for two men, halfe is	08	00	
Fiue ells coorse Canuase, to make a bed at Sea for two men, to be filled with straw, iiij.s.			
One coorse Rug at Sea for two men, will cost vj. s. is for one	05	00	
	04	00	00
Victuall.			
Eight bushels of Meale	02	00	00
Two bushels of pease at 3.s.		06	00
Two bushels of Oatemeale 4.s. 6.d.		09	00
One gallon of Aquauitæ		02	06
One gallon of Oyle		03	06
Two gallons of Vineger 1.s.		02	00
	03	03	00
Armes.			
One Armour compleat, light		17	00
One long Peece, fiue foot or fiue and a halfe, neere Musket bore	OI	02	
One sword		05	
One belt		OI	
One bandaleere		OI	06
Twenty pound of powder		18	00
Sixty pound of shot or lead, Pistoll and Goose shot		05	00
	03	09	06

	li.	s.	d.
Tooles.			
Fiue broad howes at 2.s. a piece		IO	00
Fiue narrow howes at 16.d. a piece		06	08
Two broad Axes at 3.s. 8.d. a piece		07	04
Fiue felling Axes at 18.d. a piece		07	06
Two steele hand sawes at 16.d. a piece		02	08
Two two-hand-sawes at 5. s. a piece		IO	00
One whip-saw, set and filed with box, file, and wrest		IO	00
Two hammers 12.d. a piece		02	00
Three shouels 18.d. a piece		04	06
Two spades at 18.d. a piece		03	00
Two augers 6.d. a piece		OI	00
Six chissels 6.d. a piece		03	00
Two percers stocked 4.d. a piece		00	08
Three gimlets 2.d. a piece		00	06
Two hatchets 21.d. a piece		03	06
Two froues to cleaue pale 18.d.		03	00
Two hand bills 20. a piece		03	04
One grindlestone 4.s.		04	00
Nailes of all sorts to the value of	02	00	
Two Pickaxes		03	
	06	02	08
Houshold Implements.			
One Iron Pot	∞	7	
One kettle		06	
One large frying-pan		02	06
One gridiron		OI	06
Two skillets		05	
One spit		02	
Platters, dishes, spoones of wood		04	
	OI	08	00
For Suger, Spice, and fruit, and at Sea for 6.men.	∞	12	06

So the full charge of Apparrell, Victuall, Armes, Tooles,
and houshold stuffe, and after this rate for each person,
will amount vnto about the summe of

	li.	s.	d.
	12	10	00
The passage of each man is	06	00	00
The fraight of these prouisions for a man, will bee about halfe a Tun, which is	OI	10	00
So the whole charge will amount to about	20	00	00

For a family of 6. persons and so after the rate for more.

For a family of 6. persons, and so for more or lesse after the rate.

Nets, hookes, lines, and a tent must be added, if the number of people be greater, as also some kine.

And this is the vsuall proportion that the Virginia Company do
bestow vpon their Tenants which they send.

Apparrell for one man, and so after the rate for more.

For a whole yeere for one man, and so for more after the rate.

For one man, but if halfe of your men haue armour it is sufficient so that all haue Peeces and swords.

Whosoeuer transports himselfe or any other at his owne charge vnto *Virginia*, shall for each person so transported before Midsummer 1625
haue to him and his heires for euer fifty Acres of Land vpon a first, and fifty Acres vpon a second diuision.

Imprinted at London by FELIX KYNGSTON. 1622.

A broadside advising the essential equipment needed by settlers on
the first frontier. *Courtesy, Folger Library.*

An early advertisement for Virginia tobacco. Courtesy, *Imperial Tobacco Co., Bristol, England.*

A few years later John Rolfe, who married the Indian princess Pocahontas, introduced a species of tobacco from South America or the Caribbean that was sweeter and less astringent than the native Virginia variety. From then onward, the colonists had a salable commodity in the European market, and they could think of an assured means of making a living from the soil. In the meantime, the settlers gained the right to own land which they would farm for their profit. The way to a settled way of life was open. Tobacco proved immensely profitable. Books were written to prove that it possessed medical virtues, too, and would cure many of man's diseases—as well as prove a solace and comfort.

The northern colonies—Plymouth and Massachusetts Bay—discovered that fishing and fur trading promised greater profits than farming, for the soil of New England, except in a few fertile river valleys, was rocky and thin. The sea in the North took the place of plantations in the South, and the forests supplied timbers for ships, which became an important source of revenue in New England, both for shipbuilders who sold them and for fishermen and traders who used them. Farming was important in New England, to be sure, but it was subsistence farming. Fishermen and traders grew food grains and raised cattle, sheep,

Yale College, about 1830. From an engraving by W. H. Bartlett and J. Sands. *Courtesy, Library of Congress.*

and hogs for their own use and frequently sold surplus foodstuffs to others.

Forest products, foodstuffs from farms, fish, and furs became the staples that brought prosperity to settlements in New England and to other northern colonies. The fur trade first lured the Dutch to Manhattan. And in the Far South, furs, deerskins, and forest products largely accounted for the success of colonization in the Carolinas.

During the seventeenth and early eighteenth centuries, English settlers, who gained a foothold on the Atlantic seaboard from South Carolina to Maine, gradually established a settled and civilized way of life as nearly like that in the mother country as they could make it. They had churches and a certain number of schools. The two first colleges, Harvard (1636) in Massachusetts and the College of William and Mary (1693) in Virginia, provided the elements of higher education and assured the country of a supply of preachers. Yale (1701), the third college founded, continued the tradition of training preachers and proved even more conservative than Harvard. Many years later, Dartmouth (1769), established in the backcountry of New Hampshire, was more strictly a frontier college, like many that were to follow as immigrants marched across the North American continent. Harvard, William and Mary, and Dartmouth had illusions about educating the Indians and made some attempts in that direction but soon abandoned their efforts as hopeless. Few Indians were interested in Latin or theology.

Here and there towns developed with some slight claim to Old World sophistication: Boston, New York, Philadelphia, Newport, and Charleston. These towns were important centers of commerce and helped stimulate trade with a backcountry that became the new frontier. Virginia planters, not the mere silken aristocrats that romantic fiction has made them, also sent trading expeditions into the Indian country and across the mountains in search of furs. William Byrd, the first of his name in Virginia, built a plantation center at Westover on the James River and developed a prosperous Indian trade with the interior.

During the first century of settlement along the Atlantic

The Westover Mansion at the time of the Civil War. From an engraving after a painting by E. L. Henry. *Courtesy, Library of Congress.*

The first barrier—the mountains of Virginia. From a lithograph after E. Beyer (1857). *Courtesy, Library of Congress.*

seaboard, Indian traders pushed up river valleys, passed the line of rapids and falls that blocked the navigation of ships, and penetrated into the forest areas beyond in search of furs, a commodity that never glutted the European market. The fur trade was the incentive for early Western exploration, and it remained one of the prime reasons for the penetration of the West for generations to come. Almost every type of adventurer, from aristocrat and nobleman to fugitives from the law, at one time or another engaged in the fur trade. The mountain men who helped open trails to the Far West had predecessors in the seventeenth and eighteenth centuries who showed the way to passes in the Alleghenies and led pioneers into grassy valleys and rich woodlands beyond the mountains. To the fur trade, then, we must give the credit for the development of the first frontiers beyond the limits of the Atlantic settlements.

20

2

Over the Mountains and Beyond

SETTLERS along the Atlantic seaboard found no charm
in scenery that was later to attract tourists and visitors.
Waterfalls, forests, and mountains were obstructions and
hazards that blocked their progress. A dense growth of trees
might be proof of fertile soil beneath, but these same trees
also hid dangerous animals and savage men. Death lurked in
the shadows of the woods, and no poetic Longfellows
talked of the grandeur of the murmuring pines and the
hemlocks. The magnificent rivers that cut the coastal plain
served the uses of navigation as far as the fall line, that
point where rocks and rapids prevented the passage of
ships. Beautiful as the plunging water might seem to later
generations, the rapids hindered navigation and proved an
annoyance and a loss to our ancestors. In places they could
use the flow of water to turn the wheels of their flour, grist,
and saw mills, but at first the rapids were an unmitigated
nuisance that impeded movement beyond the fall line.

The mountains still farther inland were even more of a
hindrance—unknown, mysterious, and forbidding. What
their coves and valleys might offer, few adventurers were

Running the rapids at the fall line. From a wood engraving in *Harper's Weekly* (February 21, 1874).

daring enough to discover. Although our Eastern mountains—the Allegheny escarpment and lower ranges nearer the coast—have no Alpine peaks, nevertheless, to the explorers who ventured that far in the seventeenth century, they were a formidable barrier. The lower hillsides for the most part were a tangle of undergrowth, dense and nearly impenetrable. Even valleys and flat plains were frequently overgrown with briers and vines. To pioneers of the seventeenth century, nature was less than kind as they tried to push into the interior of a continent whose extent was still unknown to them. Where not even an Indian trail existed, progress was slow and difficult.

In spite of dangers and natural barriers, a few men had the courage to probe the river valleys in search of passages to regions beyond. A belief existed that the land barrier was narrow, and across the mountains lay the Great South Sea—the ocean route to China and the East. Columbus believed that he had found islands off the China coast, and men still hoped to find a waterway leading to the

Pacific or at least a short land passage to the sea. Some of the first explorers who looked westward from the crest of the Blue Ridge convinced themselves that they saw water glimmering in the distance. One or two thought they saw sails receding in the fog. No one had any concept of a vast continent, some 3,000 miles in width, separating the Atlantic from the Pacific.

The dream of profits from trade, rather than geographical curiosity, sent explorers up the rivers and into the mountains beyond the first settlements on the Atlantic seaboard. Captain John Smith, best remembered for his story of being rescued by Pocahontas, helped show Englishmen that the fur trade might bring returns surpassing the profits from gold and silver mines. In 1614 he cruised along the coast of New England, observed enormous schools of fish, and recommended fishing as a profitable industry to his countrymen. He also did some trading with the Indians and carried home a valuable cargo of furs. His *Description of New England*, published in 1616, stressed both fish and furs as commodities that Englishmen might turn to good account. From this time onward, settlers along the Atlantic seaboard tried with varying success to develop the Indian trade.

In the Far North the French early realized that the fur trade with the Indians would be a source of enormous profit, and the French government sought to stimulate this trade at the expense of other colonizing efforts. Frenchmen pushed into the interior, sometimes became adopted members of Indian tribes, took Indian squaws to wife, learned their languages, and became important factors in the development of the fur trade. These men, known as *coureurs de bois* ("wood runners"), discovered Indian trading routes in the North, exerted considerable influence on the Northern tribes, and directed fur-laden canoes of the Indians to Montreal, Quebec, and other French trading posts. Englishmen were later to compete with the French for Northern furs; the wars that wracked the colonies in the

23

eighteenth century had as one of their objectives the control of the Indian fur trade.

The earliest English trade with the Indians of the interior region—that new frontier opening in the foothills and mountains—began in the South with explorers from the Virginia Tidewater country. The details are vague and the personalities often shadowy, for traders did not advertise their success lest they attract competitors. The first traders to leave authentic accounts of visits to the Alleghenies reported finding initials cut in the bark of trees by unknown explorers who had preceded them. From the mid-seventeenth century on, a few enterprising individuals broached the mountain barrier and began the development of a fur trade that promised wealth.

One of the earliest of these was Abraham Wood, called in Virginia history variously Captain Wood, Colonel Wood, and Major General Wood. At the falls of the Appomattox River, where the town of Petersburg now stands, Wood established a fort and trading post that became an important center for exploration and for commerce with the Indians. The colony of Virginia was anxious to have a fort on the frontier, but since it would be costly to maintain a military establishment, the legislative assembly in 1646 passed an act giving the fort on the Appomattox to Wood, along with 600 acres of land "for him and his heirs forever, with all houses and edifices belonging to the said fort, with all boats and ammunition at present belonging to the said fort, provided that he, the said Capt. Wood, do maintain and keep ten men constantly upon the said place for the term of three years during which time he, the said Capt. Wood, is exempted from all public taxes for himself and the said ten persons."[1] The colony proposed to garrison its frontier with this and other similar forts owned and occupied by private traders. Wood's post was named Fort Henry.

William Byrd I established a trading post and some sort of fortified place at the falls of the James River near the site of present-day Richmond. From this point he, too, sent traders into the backcountry with guns, powder, shot, rum, knives, hatchets, pots, kettles, blankets, gay-colored cloth, bells, and beads—trading goods used on the frontier for two centuries to come. From the Indians the traders obtained pelts of beaver, muskrats, mink, and other small fur-bearing animals. They brought back an occasional bearskin or buffalo robe. Deerskins were also in demand, and farther south, deerskins became an important article of commerce.

Another trader, Cadwallader Jones, who operated in much the same fashion as Wood and Byrd, established a fort on the Rappahannock River. Jones sent his men hundreds of miles into the wilds of present-day North and South Carolina and reaped a rich harvest of furs and skins from this virgin land.

Many years later, William Byrd II, in his *History of the Dividing Line . . . Run in . . . 1728*, described the method of trading carried on by his father, Wood, Jones, and others. Byrd and his party, surveying the boundary between Virginia and North Carolina, had crossed the trail followed by the traders who made contact with Indians in North and South Carolina, and he commented:

The trading path above-mentioned receives its name from being the route the traders take with their caravans when they go to traffic with the Catawbas and other southern Indians. The Catawbas live about 250 miles beyond the Roanoke River, and yet our traders find their account in transporting goods from Virginia to trade with them at their own town. The common method of carrying on this Indian commerce is as follows: gentlemen send for goods proper for such a trade from England and then either venture them out at their own risk to the Indian towns or else credit some traders with them of substance and reputation, to be paid in skins at [a] certain price agreed betwixt them. The goods for the Indian trade consist chiefly in guns, powder, shot, hatchets (which the Indians call

Making camp on a North Carolina trail, near Fayetteville. From an engraving in J. Shaw, *Picturesque Views of American Scenery* (1820).

tomahawks), kettles, red and blue planes [plain cloth], Duffields [coarse woolen cloth], Stroudwater blankets, and some cutlery wares, brass rings, and other trinkets.

These wares are made up into packs and carried upon horses, each load being from 150 to 200 pounds, with which they are able to travel about twenty miles a day if forage happen to be plentiful. Formerly a hundred horses have been employed in one of these Indian caravans under the conduct of fifteen or sixteen persons only, but now the trade is much impaired, insomuch that they seldom go with half that number.[2]

Byrd knew at firsthand about this frontier trade, for his father had laid the foundation of a substantial fortune by such commerce with the Indians.

Abraham Wood, owner and commander of Fort Henry, was no stay-at-home operator but was himself an explorer of the Western country. In August, 1650, he and three associates, Edward Bland, Sackford Brewster, and Elias Pennant, with two white servants and an Indian guide, set out from Fort Henry on a journey to open trade with the Tuscarora Indians to the southwest. Although Indian tribes became more and more unfriendly as they pushed farther into the wilderness, they reached a point on what was later to be the North Carolina border before turning back.

The well-watered land of rolling hills and plains, covered with oaks, hickory, poplar, ash, and pines, abounded with game. They thought it a different country from Virginia, and when, in 1651, Bland published in London an account of their journey, he called his book *The Discovery of New Brittaine*. He quoted from Sir Walter Raleigh's *Marrow of History* a statement that the earthly paradise was located on the thirty-fifth parallel of north latitude, the approximate location of New Britain. In a preface to the reader Bland urged anyone:

that desirest the advancement of God's glory by conversion of the Indians, the augmentation of the English commonwealth in extending its liberties . . . to consider the present benefit and future profits that will arise in well settling Virginia's confines, especially the happy country of New Britain in the latitude of thirty-five and thirty-seven degrees, of more temperate climate than that the English now inhabit, abounding with great rivers of long extent, and encompassing a great part or most of Virginia's continent, a place so easy to be settled in, in regard that horse and cattle in four or five days may be conveyed . . . and all inconveniences avoided which commonly attend new plantations, being supplied with necessaries from the neighborhood of Virginia.[3]

Tobacco will grow larger in New Britain than in Virginia, Bland asserted; sugarcane is indigenous, and the Indians produce two crops of corn each year; rivers provide abundant fish; silver and copper are indicated by the silver tips of the Indians' pipes and the copper plates they wear about their necks. In short, a rich and fertile land cries out for settlers. This frontier, like each new frontier that would open for generations to come, seemed fairer and richer than the country where prospective pioneers then resided. Always in North America the country beyond the

27

line of established civilization beckoned, and adventurers were always ready to heed the enticements of new land waiting to be taken.

Wood continued to encourage and promote exploration of the interior for years after his and Bland's expedition. Some of the men sent out from Fort Henry crossed the mountains and observed rivers flowing westward into the Ohio and Mississippi. How far these adventurers reached, no one knows, but they certainly learned something about the rivers of the West. William Byrd's traders also heard rumors of the waters in the Northwest later known as the Great Lakes.

Reports of the profits to be made from the Indian trade and of vast tracts of fertile land ready to be seized stirred the greed of men in the highest circles of Charles II's government. In 1663 a group including Sir William Berkeley, who had long served as royal governor of Virginia, the Earl of Clarendon, Lord Ashley (later the Earl of Shaftesbury), and five others obtained from the king a charter that made them lords proprietors of Carolina, a territory south of Virginia extensive enough to enrich them all.

The ambitions of these speculators had no bounds, and they were soon eagerly listening to two renegade French adventurers, Pierre Esprit Radisson, and his brother-in-law, Médart Chouart, who called himself the Sieur des Groseilliers. The Frenchmen had gone westward from the headwaters of the St. Lawrence River as far as Lake Superior. They had either visited or had heard from the Indians about Hudson Bay, a sea route that would outflank the St. Lawrence and open up a trade with Western Indians rich beyond the dreams of avarice. Radisson and Groseilliers knew whereof they spoke, because they had brought back to Quebec from Lake Superior a string of sixty fur-laden canoes—and, instead of being praised for their enterprise, they had received a reprimand and a heavy fine from the French government for trading without a license.

Soured by this treatment, they made their way to London

Voyageurs on Lake Superior. From an engraving after a painting by F. A. Hopkins (c. 1870). *Courtesy, Library of Congress.*

and proposed to show the English how to reach this new frontier. Although the English noblemen who heard Radisson and Groseilliers were busy with schemes to develop the Carolinas, they lost no time in beginning plans that culminated in the founding of the Hudson's Bay Company by royal charter in 1670. From this time on, English traders competed with the French for beaver and marten taken by Indian trappers of the Great Lakes region.

Another route used by English traders into the continent's interior followed the Hudson River and its tributaries to their sources. On the southern flank of French Canada the English tried to intercept the rich Indian trade that focused on Montreal and Quebec. By cementing alliances

The baronet (Sir William Johnson) in council with the Mohawks. From a wood engraving after W. L. Sheppard in A. L. Mason, *The Romance and Tragedy of Pioneer Life* (1883).

with the Iroquois, traditional enemies of the Algonquins of the North, English traders managed to gain a foothold in western New York and to make Albany an important outpost of the fur trade.

But before they could do this, they had to seize the colony from the Dutch, who had established themselves on Manhattan and in the Hudson Valley. Some of the same noble speculators who were interested in the Carolinas and a bit later in the Hudson's Bay Company were behind the movement to seize New Netherland from the Dutch. This they accomplished in 1664 with forces sent out by the Duke of York. Now an enormous new frontier reached by a magnificent river system lay open to Englishmen. Thousands of frontiersmen in the future would pass through western New York on their way to fresh lands.

From the time of the settlement of Plymouth onward, New Englanders had pushed into the backcountry in pursuit of trade or in search of better land. Captain Miles Standish in 1621 had led an expedition from Plymouth as far as Boston Harbor and had come back with a supply of beaver and otter skins. New Englanders never afterward neglected the fur trade. Groups that went out from Massachusetts Bay to settle on the Connecticut River, at Hartford, Springfield, and other sites, frequently found fur trading more lucrative than farming. Pioneers continued to advance along New England's rivers, the Connecticut, the Merrimack, and others which led them to the frontier, where they had to compete with Dutch traders for the Indians' furs and where they stood in constant danger from raids by hostile Indians instigated by the French. Deerfield, one of the most distant outposts in Massachusetts, suffered more than once from devastating attacks by Indians. In 1704 some fifty of the inhabitants were massacred, and others were taken as prisoners to Canada. But the danger of death from the tomahawks of marauding Indians could not stop the tide of pioneers who continued to pour into the backcountry.

The Dutch in Albany: house of the early governors. The architecture of New York State today retains much of this stepped-gable influence. From a lithograph by Cirpenne after a drawing by J. H. Milbert (1828). *Courtesy, Library of Congress.*

With the establishment of William Penn's proprietary colony of Pennsylvania in 1682, still another way was opened to the West. Penn made a number of treaties with the Indians and sought to keep the peace by buying their lands and respecting their hunting rights. Although the Pennsylvania authorities could not prevent all hostilities on the frontier, their negotiations with the Indians opened up large tracts of land in the interior for settlement by German and Scottish immigrants, who swarmed through the port of Philadelphia in the late seventeenth and early eighteenth centuries.

The Germans, the first to arrive, settled on fertile land near Philadelphia and in what is now Lancaster County and spread out from there. Eventually many of these Germans made their way up the river valleys, crossed the mountains, and filtered into the hinterland of Maryland and Virginia. Excellent farmers and artisans, they devel-

A door in Old Deerfield, Massachusetts. Preserved in a museum, this door still bears the deep cuts made by tomahawks in the Massacre of 1704. Courtesy, The Pioneer Valley Memorial Association.

oped prosperous communities, grew crops of grain, raised cattle, and added to their incomes by manufacturing articles of everyday use: woodenware, leather, furniture, wagons, and the famous long rifle, later to be known as the Kentucky rifle. This became the characteristic weapon of the frontiersman. No picture of Daniel Boone and his kind is complete without such a rifle.

The Scottish immigrants followed the Germans and pushed on beyond them to a more distant—and a more dangerous—frontier. They were hardy, courageous, and uncontaminated by the pacifist doctrines to which many of the Germans subscribed. Willing to equate the Indians with the Canaanites, these Scots were ready to slay them and take their land—all with Biblical authority. Many of the mountain men in the early nineteenth-century explorations of the Far West were also Scots or descendants of Scots. They made ideal frontiersmen, for they were tough and unafraid and could endure incredible hardships. With only a rifle, an ax, a knife, and a few crude tools, they were ready to start for the wilderness, confident that they could live off the country, chop down a few trees, build a shelter, and make a new homestead in the clearing. Scottish pioneers spearheaded the drive into western Pennsylvania, and in the eighteenth century they were found on most of

the other frontiers. Some of them became professional hunters and trappers, others engaged in trade with the Indians
at distant outposts, and still others took their families into
the wilderness, cleared lands, and turned to farming.

The first habitations of these frontiersmen were mere
brush shelters, less weathertight than an Indian's wigwam.
If fortunate, the frontiersman had a bearskin in which he
could roll up on the earthen floor. As he had time to spare
from hunting, woodcutting, or working his fields, he built
a more substantial cabin with a chimney made of mud and
sticks. His furniture was simple: a few wooden benches, a
crude table, perhaps a wooden frame with leather
thongs stretched across to hold a bedtick stuffed with moss,
grass, or corn shucks. Wooden pegs around the log walls
held such clothing and utensils as he possessed. A black iron
pot or two and a skillet, used over the open fire, served for
kitchenware. A wooden water bucket completed his household equipment. Life for frontiersmen—and their families,
if any—was simple and hard. But somehow they endured
the rigors of wilderness life, gradually improved their

A Conestoga wagon that crossed Pennsylvania to Lake Erie in 1813.
From a photograph by Ware Bros. Co. (c. 1913). *Courtesy, Library
of Congress.*

Indian massacre at Wilkes-Barre—on the Pennsylvania frontier. From an engraving by J. Rogers after a painting by F. O. C. Darley. Courtesy, Library of Congress.

condition, added a few more items for their comfort, and bought an occasional item of sheer luxury from a peddler, such as a mouth organ or a Jew's harp.

By the early eighteenth century, homesteaders, hunters, and traders had made a beginning at opening the West from South Carolina to Maine. This early West was an irregular zone that zigzagged through the foothills and mountains with occasional fortified outposts, usually on the headwaters of rivers. Dotted here and there beyond even these outposts were the clearings of settlers who dared to risk loneliness, isolation, and danger from Indian attacks to hew out a place for themselves in the virgin wilderness.

The most picturesque and romantic of the early frontiersmen were the fur traders, wherever they were found, from Hudson Bay to Charleston, South Carolina. They were the ones who penetrated farthest into the Indian country, risked more, and came back with the most colorful tales.

Few adventurers equaled the record of Henry Woodward, an Englishman from Barbados, who in 1666 volunteered to live among the Indians on the South Carolina coast to learn their language and ways. The knowledge gained by this experience enabled Woodward to become a successful trader and a backwoods diplomat, who for a time helped keep peace between the Indians and the colony established at Charleston.

While Woodward was living among the Indians in 1666, Spaniards from St. Augustine captured him and took him to Florida. From his captors he learned enough about medicine to call himself a surgeon. When an English buccaneer, Robert Searles, raided the Florida coast two years later, Woodward escaped and joined his ship but was wrecked on the island of Nevis in 1669. He managed to join the fleet sailing with settlers for Charleston in 1670 and from that time onward made that colony his base of operations.

Woodward contrived to make a peace pact with the much-feared Westo Indians, who occupied the lower reaches of the Savannah River, and to open trade with them. Although a few years later the South Carolinians had to go to war with the Westos, Woodward's efforts assured the colonists a profitable trade until hostilities ended it. Woodward's greatest contributions to the Carolina colony were his exploration of regions beyond the Savannah River in what became Georgia and Alabama and his es-

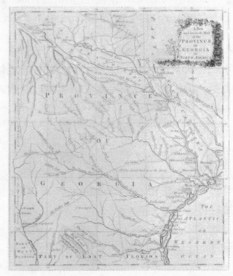

Pathways of the Indian trade in Georgia. From an eighteenth century map in the collections of the Huntington Library.

tablishment of a trade in furs, skins, and Indian slaves with the Creeks and Chickasaws of the interior. By the beginning of the eighteenth century the French in Louisiana had discovered to their sorrow that Carolina traders had already reached the lower Mississippi and, east of the river, had won over the Indians, who favored English traders over either the French or the Spanish.

Even before the turn of the century, adventurous explorers from Carolina had advanced through the woods and swamps of the lower Mississippi as far as the mouth of the Arkansas River. They carried presents to the Indians, bought their peltries for a fair price, and won their friendship. The enterprise of the English greatly alarmed the French, who foresaw an end of their influence with the tribes on the eastern side of the Mississippi. News of favorable opportunities for trade with the English even reached a few of the French *coureurs de bois,* who brought packs of furs to English trading houses in South Carolina. The French were never able to dislodge the Carolina traders from the eastern flank of Louisiana; these hardy pioneers had reached the West and were determined to stay.

News of the opportunities in this new territory created excitement in Great Britain and stirred a Welshman of property and standing, Price Hughes of Montgomeryshire, to launch a scheme to settle a Welsh colony on the lower Mississippi. Unfortunately, Hughes was murdered in Louisiana in 1715, and his death brought an end to one of the earliest projects to populate trans-Appalachia with British subjects.

Another territory that proved valuable for trade lay to the northwest of Carolina in the foothills and mountains. A powerful Indian nation, the Cherokees, dominated this region. A proud and intelligent people, they for many years proved useful, if difficult, allies of the English. Traders from Charleston made their way along a trail that led up the eastern bank of the Savannah River until they reached the highlands of the Cherokees. There they bar-

36

Intertribal warfare: Assiniboin attack on a Blackfoot village at Fort Mackenzie on the upper Missouri, August 28, 1833. From an aquatint after C. Bodmer, in Maximilian Wied-Neuwied, *Travels in the Interior of North America, the Atlas* (1843–44). Bernard De Voto has described Bodmer's picture as one of the best studies ever made of Indian warfare.

tered for deerskins—and sometimes for slaves captured from other tribes by the Cherokees. These slaves they took back to Charleston, where merchants shipped them to the West Indies; they could not be used by Carolina planters because they too easily escaped into the forests.

The traders who followed the Cherokee trail and those who journeyed farther still into the Southwest were a tough lot. They usually made a rendezvous in Charleston in the spring of the year. Long trains of packhorses with tinkling bells clattered over the cobbled streets to unload their burdens of deerskins, beaver pelts, and other furs at warehouses on the Charleston docks. The traders themselves, many of them as bronzed and weatherbeaten as Indians, swarmed into taverns and used the profits of a long winter's work in one grand carousal. At last, sober and in need of funds, they loaded trading goods on packhorses and again set out for the Indian country.

Some of the traders were careful to keep peace with the Indians by fair dealing; others were not above plying them with rum and tricking them out of their furs. Friction be-

37

tween Indians and traders was frequent and sometimes ended in violence and murder. Although the governments in all the colonies attempted to control contacts with the Indians by licensing the traders, once a trader had left for the Indian country, no authority could watch him and police his conduct.

The Indians, on their part, were suspicious and often treacherous. Furthermore, incessant warfare between the tribes caught the traders in the middle. If they took sides, they incurred the lasting hatred of the tribes they opposed. Consequently, the life of a trader was hazardous, and many of them died at the hands of the Indians, sometimes after hideous torture. Contemporary accounts tell of the Indians slowly roasting their victims to death, after pulling out their fingernails and sticking their bodies full of burning splinters.

Rivalry between individual free traders and between the agents of wealthy operators like William Byrd I and Abraham Wood was always intense and sometimes led to violence. Competition between traders from the separate colonies also caused much hard feeling and some official complaint by colonial authorities. For example, the Virginians sent trading caravans into Catawba and Cherokee territory, which the Carolinians regarded as their special preserves. New Englanders and Marylanders sometimes invaded the backcountry of Virginia. All the English traders hated the French and the Spaniards. And all the rival groups tried to outwit the others and monopolize the trade when they could.

Profits to be made out of the fur trade and the greed of Sir William Berkeley, governor of Virginia, helped bring on a frontier uprising led in 1676 by Nathaniel Bacon, Jr. At this time the frontiers of Virginia beyond the fall line of the rivers were subject to frequent Indian attack; the settlers believed that Berkeley was so concerned lest border fighting disturb the fur trade that he would not permit adequate retaliation against the Indians for ravaging outlying settlements. Taking the law into their hands, these frontiersmen, urged on by Bacon, drove the Indians from the borders and made the settlements relatively safe again. But flushed with these victories, they then sought to overturn Berkeley's government at Jamestown. In the midst of the uproar Bacon died, and the rebellion fizzled out. The border warfare, however, with which Bacon's Rebellion started, was characteristic of conflicts between settlers and Indians that would rage on many frontiers in the generations to come.

By 1700 Indian traders had probed the mountains and backcountry from South Carolina to Canada and had brought back information that whetted the appetite of land-hungry speculators in both the colonies and the mother country. The next two generations would see a constant stream of settlers flowing into rich valleys of the hinterland and struggling across mountain ridges to territory even more distant.

Governor Alexander Spotswood of Virginia in 1716 led a famous exploring expedition over the Blue Ridge Mountains to a point on the Shenandoah River (which he called the Euphrates) in the Valley of Virginia near present-day Elkton. Fortunately, Spotswood had as one of his group of convivial companions a careful observer and a diary keeper, young John Fontaine, who left a vivid account of the activities of the explorers. The party, consisting of sixty-three men, including scouts, Indian guides, and servants, gathered at Spotswood's own frontier mining settlement of Germanna on the Rapidan River on August 24. From there they set out, following the Rapidan and later the Swift Run through Swift Run Gap and down on the west side of the Blue Ridge to the Shenandoah. Although Spotswood had a serious purpose and hoped to open up new territory for trade and settlement, he and his party took time for hunting and fishing and for merry evenings around the campfire at which they consumed enormous quantities of liquor of various sorts.

Rarely have any explorers carried a better "cellar" than that which Spotswood loaded on his packhorses. After a day struggling through vines and briers, risking rattlesnake and copperhead bites, and fighting off flies and mosquitoes, the explorers needed refreshment. They washed down venison and bear steaks with excellent wine. When they attained the summit of the Blue Ridge on September 5, they "drank King George's health and the Royal Family's," Fontaine reports. That night on the Shenandoah they continued their celebration. The next day they crossed the river and buried a bottle containing a paper on which Spotswood wrote out a claim to the land in the name of King George I. Fontaine described that evening's festivities: "We had a good dinner and after it we got the men together and loaded all their arms, and we drank the King's health in champagne, and fired a volley; the Princess' health in burgundy, and fired a volley; and all the rest of the Royal Family in claret, and a volley. We had several sorts of liquors, viz., Virginia red and white wine, Irish usquebaugh [whiskey], brandy, shrub, two sorts of rum, champagne, canary, cherry, punch, water, cider, etc. I sent two of the rangers to look for my gun, which I dropped in the mountains; they found it, and brought it to me at night, and I gave them a pistole for their trouble." With that much drink, it is no wonder that Fontaine lost his gun.

Nevertheless, the expedition was something more than a late summer's holiday. Spotswood's examination of the Valley of Virginia convinced him and his colleagues of the value of the country beyond the mountains and made the Virginians determined to hold it against the incursions of the French from Canada.

Not all the explorations of the hinterland were as successful as Spotswood's or could boast the pleasures experienced by his reveling gentlemen of Virginia. But every new journey into the interior by trapper or explorer added a bit of knowledge about a vast and fascinating land beyond the mountain barriers. English dwellers on the coast

40

came to believe that the West held out a hope of new wealth for those with the strength and courage to make the venture. Early in colonial times adventurous youth began to dream of seeking their fortunes in the West, and that dream would persist until modern times.

William Byrd Tells of Frontier Life in North Carolina (1728)

William Byrd II, of Westover, Virginia, led a party that surveyed the border between Virginia and North Carolina in 1728. His *History of the Dividing Line,* first published in 1841, gives an amusing account of the surveying party's adventures on this early frontier. The most recent version is found in *The Prose Works of William Byrd of Westover,* edited by Louis B. Wright and published by the Harvard University Press, 1966. The passage below gives Byrd's views of life in the North Carolina backcountry.

Surely there is no place in the world where the inhabitants live with less labor than in North Carolina. It approaches nearer to the description of Lubberland than any other, by the great felicity of the climate, the easiness of raising provisions, and the slothfulness of the people. Indian corn is of so great increase that a little pains will subsist a very large family with bread, and then they may have meat without any pains at all, by the help of the low grounds and the great variety of mast that grows on the high land. The men, for their parts, just like the Indians, impose all the work upon the poor women. They make their wives rise out of their beds early in the morning, at the same time that they lie and snore till the sun has risen one-third of his course and dispersed all the unwholesome damps. Then, after stretching and yawning for half an hour, they light their pipes, and, under the protection of a cloud of smoke, venture out into the open air; though if it happen to be never so little cold they quickly return shivering into the chimney corner. When the weather is mild they stand leaning with both their arms upon the cornfield fence and gravely consider whether they had best

41

go and take a small heat at the hoe but generally find reasons to put it off till another time. Thus they loiter away their lives, like Solomon's sluggard, with their arms across, and at the winding up of the year scarcely have bread to eat. To speak the truth, 'tis a thorough aversion to labor that makes people file off to North Carolina, where plenty and a warm sun confirm them in their disposition to laziness for their whole lives.

Since we were like to be confined to this place till the people returned out of the Dismal [swamp], 'twas agreed that our chaplain might safely take a turn to Edenton to preach the Gospel to the infidels there and christen their children. He was accompanied thither by Mr. Little, one of the Carolina commissioners, who, to show his regard for the church, offered to treat him on the road with a fricassee of rum. They fried half a dozen rashers of very fat bacon in a pint of rum, both which being dished up together served the company at once both for meat and drink.

Most of the rum they get in this country comes from New England and is so bad and unwholesome that it is not improperly called "kill-devil." It is distilled there from foreign molasses, which, if skillfully managed, yields near gallon for gallon. Their molasses comes from the same country and has the name of "long sugar" in Carolina, I suppose from the ropiness of it, and serves all the purposes of sugar, both in their eating and drinking. When they entertain their friends bountifully, they fail not to set before them a capacious bowl of bombo, so called from the admiral of that name. This is a compound of rum and water in equal parts, made palatable with the said long sugar. As good humor begins to flow and the bowl to ebb they take care to replenish it with sheer rum, of which there always is a reserve under the table.

But such generous doings happen only when that balsam of life is plenty; for they have often such melancholy times that neither landgraves nor caciques can procure one drop for their wives when they lie in or are troubled with the colic or vapors. Very few in this country have the industry to plant orchards, which, in a dearth of rum, might supply them with much better liquor. The truth is, there is one inconvenience that easily discourages lazy people from making this improvement: very often, in autumn, when the apples begin to ripen, they are visited with numerous flights of parakeets, that bite all the fruit to pieces in a moment for the sake of the kernels. The havoc they make is sometimes so great that whole orchards are laid waste, in spite of all the noises that can be made or mawkins [scarecrows] that can be dressed up to fright 'em away. These ravenous birds visit North Carolina only during the warm season and so soon as the cold begins to come on retire back toward the sun. They rarely venture so far north as Virginia, except in a very hot summer, when they visit the most southern parts of it. They are very beautiful but, like some other pretty creatures, are apt to be loud and mischievous.

Betwixt this [plantation] and Edenton there are many huckleberry slashes [swamps] which afford a convenient harbor for wolves and foxes. The first of these wild beasts is not so large and fierce as they are in other countries more northerly. He will not attack a man in the keenest of his hunger but run away from him, as from an animal more mischievous than himself. The foxes are much bolder and will sometimes not only make a stand but likewise assault anyone that would balk them of their prey. The inhabitants hereabouts take the trouble to dig abundance of wolf pits, so deep and perpendicular that when a wolf is once tempted into them he can no more scramble out again than a husband who has taken the leap can scramble out of matrimony.

Most of the houses in this part of the country are log houses, covered with pine or cypress shingles, three feet long and one broad. They are hung upon lathes with pegs, and their doors, too, turn upon wooden hinges and have wooden locks to secure them, so that the building is finished without nails or other ironwork. They also set up their pales without any nails at all, and, indeed, more securely than those that are nailed. There are three rails mortised into the posts, the lowest of which serves as a sill, with a groove in the middle big enough to receive the end of the pales; the middle part of the pale rests against the inside of the next rail, and the top of it is brought forward to the outside of the uppermost. Such wreathing of the pales in and out makes them stand firm and much harder to unfix than when nailed in the ordinary way.

Within three or four miles of Edenton the soil appears to be a little more fertile, though it is much cut with slashes, which seem all to have a tendency toward the Dismal. This town is situate on the north side of Albemarle Sound, which is there about five miles over. A dirty slash runs all along the back of it, which in the summer is a foul annoyance and furnishes abundance of that Carolina plague, mosquitoes. There may be forty or fifty houses, most of them small and built without expense. A citizen here is counted extravagant if he has ambition enough to aspire to a brick chimney. Justice herself is but indifferently lodged, the courthouse having much of the air of a common tobacco house. I believe this is the only metropolis in the Christian or Mahometan world where there is neither church, chapel, mosque, synagogue, or any other place of public worship of any sect or religion whatsoever. What little devotion there may happen to be is much more private than their vices. The people seem easy without a minister as long as they are exempted from paying him. Sometimes the Society for Propagating the Gospel has had the charity to send over missionaries to this country; but, unfortunately, the priest has been too lewd for the people, or, which oftener happens, they too lewd for the priest. For these reasons these reverend gentlemen have always left their flocks as arrant heathen as they found them. Thus much, however, may be said for the inhabitants of Edenton, that not a soul has the least taint of hypocrisy or superstition, acting very frankly and aboveboard in all their exercises.

Provisions here are extremely cheap and extremely good, so that people may live plentifully at a trifling expense. Nothing is dear but law, physic, and strong drink, which are all bad in their kind, and the last they get with so much difficulty that they are never guilty of the sin of suffering it to sour upon their hands. Their vanity generally lies not so much in having a handsome dining room as a handsome house of office: in this kind of structure they are really extravagant. They are rarely guilty of flattering or making any court to their governors but treat them with all the excesses of freedom and familiarity. They are of opinion their rulers would be apt to grow insolent if they grew rich, and for that reason take care to keep them poorer and more dependent, if possible, than the saints in New England used to do their governors. They have very little coin, so they are forced to carry on their home traffic with paper money. This is the only cash that will tarry in the country, and for that reason the discount goes on increasing between that and real money and will do so to the end of the chapter.

3

Daniel Boone
and the Kentucky Pioneers

DURING the eighteenth century the American colonies found themselves embroiled in every war that England fought with France. That meant that settlers on the exposed frontiers were in constant danger of attack from Indians allied with France. The English also had Indian allies who frequently led war parties into French territory. The result was turmoil in the backcountry through long periods in the eighteenth century. But finally, in 1763, after British victories in all quarters of the globe, France surrendered to Britain French claims to Canada and the Ohio Valley, and Great Britain signed the Treaty of Paris, which everyone hoped would establish permanent peace in North America.

Armchair statesmen in London thought they saw a way to prevent future conflicts with the Indians, stop friction between Indians and white interlopers on Indian land, and guarantee the continued prosperity of the fur trade. They

Indians plundering a South Carolina plantation. From a wood engraving by A. Bobbett after F. O. C. Darley. *Courtesy, Library of Congress.*

would draw a line along the crest of the Alleghenies and forbid white settlers to move beyond the line until they negotiated treaties with Indian tribes for the purchase of Western land. So the Proclamation Line of 1763 came into being, a line that pleased nobody, unless perhaps the authorities in faraway London liked their handiwork. In theory, the plan sounded fine. It would reserve a great area for the Indians and the fur traders; eventually, when settlers needed more land, some territories could be opened to them by treaty and purchase.

What the authorities in London forgot or refused to acknowledge was the fact that individual colonies claimed enormous areas of Western land, some all the way to the Pacific. For at least a generation before the American Revolution, speculation in Western land rose and fell like the

A map made to show the Proclamation Line of October 7, 1763.
Note the "Lands Reserved for the Indians" beyond the Alleghenies.
From *The Gentleman's Magazine* (October, 1763). Courtesy, Huntington Library.

tide, as colonists in the older settled regions dreamed of getting rich from land beyond the mountains. Land companies flourished, and like real estate operators in every age, they persuaded investors that prosperity would soon be theirs. George Washington was only one of many colonists interested in Western land. Although the Proclamation of 1763 might disturb the land companies and their clients, it did not prevent prospectors from going beyond the line and staking out claims for themselves.

Indeed, for years before 1763 the westward movement had already been under way. No sooner had the British in 1758 ousted the French from the forks of the Ohio and firmly established themselves at Fort Pitt (later Pittsburgh) in western Pennsylvania than squatters began to build cabins around the fort and to stake out land for themselves. Although an Ottawa Indian chief, Pontiac, who led an uprising of Ottawas, Shawnees, and Delawares in 1763, temporarily swept western Pennsylvania clean of white settlers, he was routed, and within five years some 2,000 white families had established themselves along the tributaries of the Ohio River in western Pennsylvania. By 1770 more than 10,000 families had settled western Pennsylvania south of the Ohio River.

Elsewhere a corresponding westward movement was taking place. Intrepid souls from Virginia and North Carolina moved through the mountains to the Watauga River Valley in what is now eastern Tennessee. Two of their leaders, James Robertson and Robert Bean, leased land from the Cherokees; the settlers presently drew up the Watauga Association, a compact designed to assure a stable society by creating a commission of five members who were to

Daniel Boone. From an engraving by J. B. Longacre after the portrait by Chester Harding (1839). *Courtesy, Library of Congress.*

Wild turkeys roosting in a tree at sunset. From a wood engraving after a drawing by T. R. Davis, in *Harper's Weekly* (February 4, 1871).

serve as the governing authorities in the Watauga settlements.

The westward movement that has attracted the greatest romantic interest of later ages, however, was the infiltration of Kentucky, principally because of episodes, real and imagined, connected with the career of the hunter and scout Daniel Boone.

Boone was not the first English colonist to hear about the rich lands of the Kentucky bluegrass. Perhaps the earliest to see the region was an Indian trader named John Finley, who was captured by the Shawnees in 1752 and kept prisoner for a time in the bluegrass country. He lived to return to civilization and to spread the word about the fertility of the soil, the abundance of game, and the mildness of the climate. During the next decade parties of hunters pushed over the mountains to the lowlands in search of deer, buffalo, wild turkeys, and other game. They all confirmed early reports about Kentucky. One of these hunters and traders, Benjamin Cutbird of North Carolina, took along Daniel Boone's brother-in-law, John Stewart, on an expedition that crossed Kentucky and northern Tennessee and eventually wound up in New Orleans, where Stewart found a ready market for furs that he had collected.

On his return to his Yadkin River settlement, Stewart told Boone about the marvels of the Western country and inflamed his brother-in-law's curiosity. Boone shouldered his rifle and set off to see for himself a land where wild turkeys were so plentiful that they broke down trees where they roosted, where every creek abounded with mink and weasels whose pelts brought money from the traders, where deer swarmed in herds. Some Indians also hunted in this region, and a man had to be wary to escape with a scalp on his head, but Boone believed that he could outwit the red man—and did.

A North Carolina land speculator named Richard Henderson staked Boone to the powder, shot, and supplies needed for his journeys in exchange for information that Boone brought back; precise facts were invaluable to promoters like Henderson, for such information might lead to the selection of rich and level lowlands instead of some inhospitable mountain wilderness. Henderson was betting on finding good land to entice emigrants and purchasers over the mountains. In 1775 Henderson organized the Transylvania Company and made a deal with the Cherokee Indians for a large principality on the Kentucky and Holston rivers. To make the land accessible, he sent Daniel Boone and a company of woodcutters to hew out a road from the Holston River through the Cumberland Gap and on to the Kentucky River. This trail, marked by stumps and fallen trees, was the Wilderness Road, over which for many years poured immigrants to what was then the Far West.

Although Henderson had obtained his land by treaty with the Cherokees, he could not keep intruders from mov-

51

ing into the territory and marking out farms for themselves. He charged only twenty shillings per 100 acres (with an annual quitrent in addition of two shillings per 100 acres), but many of the immigrants to the new country saw no reason to pay him anything when they could stake out farmlands for themselves with nobody to hinder them except marauding Indians. They expected their trusty rifles to take care of that problem.

So despite the King of England's laws and Richard Henderson's treaty with the Indians, the backcountry began to be sprinkled with little settlements of Virginians, North Carolinians, and Pennsylvanians. Much squabbling and quarreling went on over land boundaries. Finally, in 1776, under the leadership of a young frontiersman named George Rogers Clark, a convention was called at the little settlement of Harrodsburg; the delegates voted to have nothing further to do with the Transylvania Company and petitioned Virginia to take them under its protection as Kentucky County, a request that Virginia granted the next year. Kentucky now had a semblance of legality and the forms of civilized government, though it remained a wilderness harassed by Indian raids and the lawlessness characteristic of every frontier region.

The best remembered Kentuckian of this early period is, of course, Daniel Boone, whose exploits were chronicled by a contemporary schoolteacher named John Filson in a book published in 1784 with the title *The Discovery, Settlement, and Present State of Kentucke*. This work, Filson claimed, was an autobiography of Daniel Boone. Filson made Boone talk like a schoolteacher, something the barely literate Boone could never have accomplished. But in later life Boone himself was charmed by "his" narrative and claimed that every word was true.

Since the first publication of Filson's book many accounts of Boone have appeared in print, and he has become the prototype of the noble frontiersman. In our time he has appeared as the hero of a weekly television show, always

Benjamin Franklin in a coonskin cap. From an engraving by A. H. Ritchie after a drawing by C. N. Cochin made in 1777. *Courtesy, Library of Congress.*

brave, always astute and cunning, always righteous, always successful. And he still talks like a schoolteacher! He has been the hero of numerous volumes of fiction, for both adults and children. Stories of Boone have appeared in many languages. Filson's book was early translated into French and German, and the American frontiersman in coonskin cap became such a popular figure that Benjamin Franklin, serving as ambassador in Paris, capitalized on the vogue of the frontier hero by wearing a coonskin cap. Frenchmen thought all Americans from a land they still

53

thought of as wild and new must be at least part frontiersmen.

The poet Byron devoted seven stanzas in Canto 8 of *Don Juan* to Daniel Boone. Timothy Flint, an American writer who found his themes in the unfolding history of the West, wrote a volume about Boone, which he called *Biographical Memoir of Daniel Boone, the First Settler of Kentucky* (1833). Later editions appeared with the title *The First White Man of the West*.

The historical Boone, as distinct from the Boone of literature, was courageous enough in his own right and was famous in his time as a hunter and explorer. Born in 1734 in the country near Reading, Pennsylvania, the son of a man who combined the crafts of weaving and blacksmithing with farming and cattle raising, Boone was taken as a boy by his family to a settlement on the Yadkin River in the backcountry of North Carolina. He served as a teamster and blacksmith in the ill-fated expedition of General Edward Braddock against the French at Fort Duquesne in 1755, and on that journey he heard talk about Kentucky.

Although he had taken a wife, during the next ten years he was not averse to leaving her for months at a time while on hunting trips, one of which extended to Pensacola, Florida, where he wanted to settle, but where his wife refused to go. By 1767 he was off again on an extensive expedition into Kentucky, and in 1769 he left on another foray into the same alluring game country, where he stayed for two years.

Boone himself frequently went alone, but he occasionally had companions, for many hunters from North Carolina, Virginia, and Pennsylvania traveled through the Kentucky river bottoms in search of game. Because of the long periods they spent on these expeditions, they were called the long hunters. Some failed to return, for Cherokee, Shawnee, and other Indians also hunted in the same region and were not always hesitant about taking a white man's scalp. At other times the Indians contented themselves with robbing the hunters of their furs and equipment. The constant hostility between various Indians tribes and white hunters gave the region the name of the Dark and Bloody Ground.

The hunters sought furs and deerskins, which they cached in hiding places until they were ready to return to civilization. They transported their skins and furs on pack-horses or used canoes on the rivers to reach a frontier trading post. Life was always hazardous, and they could never be certain that Indians would not discover their caches and make off with a year's labor. One hunting party, returning to base and finding their furs gone, carved on a tree a record of their discontent: "2300 deerskins lost. Ruination by God."

Present-day Americans, accustomed to luxuries supplied by a supermarket, can hardly imagine the hardships encountered by these long hunters, who opened up Kentucky for the settlers following after them. Dressed in buckskin jackets, leather breeches, and moccasins, they set out on foot to cover endless miles of forest, canebrakes, weed-covered fields, and swamps. They carried few supplies, for they expected to live off the country. Each hunter cradled a long rifle in his arm and carried a flask of powder slung over his shoulder and a supply of lead bullets. He also had a knife, an ax, and a few simple tools in case he needed to mend his rifle. A canteen, a blanket, a flint and steel for making a fire, tobacco for his pipe, and perhaps a little salt were the essentials. He might start with a few pounds of flour or meal when he left the last trading post, but that was soon consumed. For the next year or longer, his rifle would supply his meat, and a canopy of pine boughs would protect him from the weather. When his clothes wore out, he would contrive to make substitutes from the hides of animals he killed. When his moccasins gave way, he would make others as the Indians did. He was as nearly self-sufficient as a human could be. So bountiful was game that he ran little risk of going hungry. Even without a gun, he could capture wild pigeons or turkeys or catch fish in the streams.

The long hunters explored the Kentucky and Ohio country and brought back information which land speculators used in staking out claims for territory later parceled out to emigrants from the settled East. Before the Revolutionary War, farmers in search of land were gradually moving into this Western country, and after the war was over, the tide of immigration increased to a flood.

The Indians did not give up their hunting grounds without a struggle. Encouraged by the British during the Revolution and even afterward, they waged bloody war on frontier settlements. Hundreds of families were wiped out in Kentucky and Ohio by marauding Indian bands, sometimes supported by British soldiers.

Finally, in the spring of 1794, General Anthony Wayne led an army of more than 2,000 men, including some 700 mounted Kentuckians, against the Indians and decisively defeated them at the Battle of Fallen Timbers on the Maumee River, not far from the Lake Erie shore. The

Danger from marauding Indians increased as the frontier moved West. From a wood engraving in *Frank Leslie's Illustrated Newspaper*, Vol. 36 (1873).

An early trading post on the Missouri—Mr. Dougherty's Agency at Bellevue. From an aquatint after Bodmer in Wied-Neuwied, *Travels in the Interior.*

next year he made a treaty of peace with various tribes in the Northwest and obtained the cession of Indian land which included Detroit, the site of Chicago, and land in Ohio, Indiana, and Illinois. Thus, the settlement of the Northwest was assured.

In the meantime, trouble with the Spaniards arose, for they had obtained the territory of Louisiana from the French and hoped to see the infant nation of the United States collapse. Some Westerners from the English colonies also were not certain that the United States would survive, and some settlers in Kentucky and Ohio talked of declaring for Spanish citizenship, which would guarantee them an outlet for their goods through the port of New Orleans. But in 1795 the United States and Spain signed the Treaty of San Lorenzo, which gave United States citizens the right of navigation on the Mississippi and an outlet through the port of New Orleans.

Crossing the Ohio to Cincinnati in 1802. From a woodcut in the collections of the Library of Congress.

Immediately after the close of the Revolutionary War, and before American soldiers had established the authority of the new nation among the Western Indians, settlers began to pour into Kentucky and Ohio. Using little posts that the hunters and early immigrants had already established—Harrodsburg, Boonesboro, and Frankfort—they spread out into the rich bluegrass country of Kentucky and quickly established new settlements: Lexington, Paris, Richmond, Danville, Louisville, and other outposts. Settlers also moved across the Ohio River. Pressure from land speculators, especially land-hungry promoters from New England, was partially responsible for Congress' passing the famous Ordinance of 1787, which established the territory northwest of the Ohio; this act opened up land for settlement north of the Ohio River and paved the way for the creation of new states. Ohio was admitted as a state in 1803. Kentucky had been admitted in 1792 and Tennessee in 1796.

The year 1788 marked a great migration to the new West, especially to Kentucky and, with somewhat less momentum, to Ohio. Kentucky speculators moved across the Ohio River and laid out a town that became Cincinnati. Another group of speculators from Connecticut, led by a pioneering preacher named Manasseh Cutler, General Rufus Putnam, and others, obtained land on the Ohio and settled the town of Marietta. Soon other towns and villages were springing up on both sides of the Ohio River in Kentucky and Ohio.

The courage and endurance of the emigrants who set out to find new homes in the territories across the Alleghenies excited the admiration of later generations. The emigrants headed for Kentucky and Ohio had to make part of their journey over miserable mountain trails, jolting along in wagons or carts or riding horseback. Even when they were out of the mountains and on level ground, the roadways were muddy tracks in wet weather and dusty trails in dry. Some of the roads followed well-worn trails made by buffalo going to salt licks in Kentucky.

Once the emigrants had reached a navigable river, they might entrust themselves and their goods to a flatboat, but navigation was hazardous. No buoys marked hidden snags and sandbars. During spring freshets, floating tree trunks and other debris might capsize or smash their flatboats. From the banks, skulking Indians sometimes fired on the boats and sneaked out in canoes to murder the passengers and make off with their goods. No easy path led to the promised lands in the West.

Contemporary letters and journals give vivid pictures of conditions that the pioneers endured, both in their travels and in the early days of settlement. Among the best accounts are letters written by Daniel Drake, later a physician, whose parents in 1788 took him, as a child of three, from New Jersey to Mayslick, Kentucky. Late in life, he wrote a series of letters to various relatives to give his recollections of pioneer days in Kentucky; these have been published in a volume, *Pioneer Life in Kentucky*. Drake reported the stories his mother and father told him about their earliest days in Kentucky, and afterward he gave his own memories of life in a frontier settlement.

An immigrant family could not look forward to comfort on arrival at their destination. No tavern or hostelry was there to welcome them. They were lucky if they could find a cleared place in the woods where they could start a new habitation. The Drakes, for example, were glad to be allowed to stay in a covered sheep pen at Mayslick until they could throw up some sort of shelter of their own.

After legal right to a grant of land had been obtained, the first task was to erect a cabin of logs, notched and fitted as close as possible together. The cracks were daubed with mud. At one end were a fireplace and a chimney made with light sticks crisscrossed to hold a filling of mud to prevent the sticks from taking fire. The mud and stick chimneys were far from safe, for the mud frequently cracked away, leaving dry sticks exposed to fire. The early cabins usually had only narrow portholes, rather than windows, and only one door, made of hewed timbers and heavily barred. The roof was covered with split timbers and

Emigrants going downriver in a flatboat. From an engraving in W. A. Crafts, *Pioneers in the Settlement of America* (1876). *Courtesy, Library of Congress.*

An idealized version of a log cabin home on the frontier. Note the deer and poultry—mainstays of frontier diet. From a lithograph by Currier & Ives (1870). *Courtesy, Library of Congress.*

shakes (rough shingles split from lengths of sawed logs). Some settlers contented themselves with earthen floors. Others had floors made of the hewn logs, laid on sleepers (crossbeams) with the flat side up.

Drake described his cabin home as a child:

For the next six years my father continued to reside at the same place in the same original log cabin, which in due course of time acquired a roof, a puncheon floor below and a clapboard roof above, a small square window without glass, and a chimney, carried up with "cats and clay" to the height of the ridgepole. These "cats and clay" were pieces of small poles well-imbedded in mortar. The rifle, indispensable both for hunting and defense, lay on two pegs driven into one of the logs. The axe and scythe . . . were kept at night under the bed as weapons of defense in case Indians should make an attack. In the morning, the first duty was to ascend a ladder leaning behind the door to the loft and look through the cracks for Indians lest they might have planted themselves near the door to rush in when the strong crossbar should be removed and the heavy latch raised from its resting place.

In some of the northern areas, maple sugar was an important product. From a Currier & Ives lithograph (1872). *Courtesy, Library of Congress.*

Until crops and vegetables could be planted, the immigrant family had to live off the country. Deer and turkeys were numerous. Drake reported that turkeys were so fat that when they fell off tree limbs where they roosted, they split open. Meat was plentiful, but despite the salt licks in the region, salt was scarce, and meat, often eaten unsalted, proved so monotonous that everyone craved bread; the children frequently cried for it.

A more balanced diet eventually became available when a family had managed to raise a crop of corn, wheat, and garden vegetables. Pumpkins, which grew to a great size, supplied sweetening. The pulp, grated and mixed with water, was boiled into a sort of molasses. Honey, taken from hollow bee trees, added to natural sweetening. Settlers with sugar maples on their land learned to tap the trees in the spring and boil the sap into maple sugar.

Among the vegetables, turnips, cabbages, peas, and beans were the staples of diet. Small boys had the responsibility of gathering hickory nuts and walnuts in the autumn and picking wild berries and plums in the summer.

Apple and peach trees came into bearing two or three years after planting. Both apples and peaches were dried in the sun for winter use. Raw turnips, which kept through the winter, were regarded as a delicacy. Drake described the family sitting around a blazing fire on a winter evening "engaged with a dull case knife in scraping and eating a sweet and juicy turnip" which made the old people forget "the pears and apples of their native Jersey."

Indian corn, however, was the staple food for both man and beast. "Neither wheat, nor rye, nor barley, nor the far-famed potato could have been substituted for the admirable maize," Drake asserted. Corn also provided the occasion for many frontier frolics—and fights. Drake described a characteristic corn shucking contest, when neighbors for miles around gathered, imbibed freely from a "green-glass quart whiskey bottle," and proceeded with a contest of cornhusking. A great pile of corn was divided in the middle by a rail, sides were chosen, and each side started husking the ears of its pile. The side finishing first, declared winner,

Combining work with pleasure—a cornhusking frolic. He who found a red ear might claim a kiss. From a wood engraving in *Harper's Weekly* (November 13, 1858).

had the privilege of marching around the vanquished shouting their victory amid further pulls on the whiskey bottle. Then everybody went to a feast prepared by the women. "Either before or after eating the fighting started," said Drake, "and by midnight the sober were found assisting the drunken home."

Husking corn was not the last labor involved before humans could use it for food. It had to be shelled by hand, a task that left blisters on many a thumb. Then it had to be ground into meal. At first, small hand mills were the only means available, but gradually water mills or horse-driven mills were established. A boy would be sent with a sack of corn thrown across the back of his horse to the nearest mill and would wait while the corn was ground. Going to mill and sitting around with others waiting for their meal offered an opportunity for gossip and storytelling that broke the monotony of isolation on frontier farms.

Clearing land for agriculture was laborious and time-consuming. Trees needed for building or firewood were cut down and dragged away with horses or oxen. But many

Bringing home firewood by an ox-drawn sleigh. From a wood engraving after a drawing by E. Forbes, in *Harper's Weekly* (January 20, 1866).

Clearing land for agriculture was laborious and time-consuming. A farmer moves large rocks from a field with the aid of a horse and sledge. From a wash drawing by A. B. Frost. *Courtesy, Library of Congress.*

trees were simply girdled with an ax and left to die. Under-brush had to be uprooted with a mattock and burned. For the first year after clearing, seed was usually planted with a hoe because fields filled with tree roots defied a plow. Cultivating new ground, as the freshly cleared land was called, remained difficult until time rotted the thickly matted roots. Fields were so rough that a boy often had to lead the horse while the plowman did his best to dodge girdled trees, stumps, and roots. For years gaunt, dead trees, waiting for winter storms to blow them down, cluttered fields. So rich was the soil, however, that even with the slightest cultivation to keep down the weeds the land produced heavy crops of corn, wheat, pumpkins, peas, beans, and turnips.

When the danger of thievery by Indians was not too great, cattle and hogs were left to roam fields, woods, and

Creating a farm out of woodland. Note the tree stumps. The canoes are birchbark; the one in the foreground is poled by an Indian male; the other paddled by Indian squaws. The various types of fences illustrated are: 4. log fence; 5. "worm" fences; 6. post-and-rail fence; 7. Virginia rail fence. From an engraving in P. Campbell, *Travels in the Interior Parts of North America* (1793).

canebrakes to forage for themselves. Owners marked pigs by clipping their ears in some special way. Cows at first were not so numerous that they required branding. Bells around their necks helped the owners locate them. Fences made of rails from wood that split easily protected cultivated fields. In Kentucky ash and honey locust trees were favored, though oak, chestnut, and pine might also furnish rails.

Rail splitting was winter work, when crops required no cultivation. The essential tools were a wooden maul and iron wedges. Stout rail fences that zigzagged across the fields would last for years, but they were not always animal-proof. Hogs had a way of rooting under even when farmers put rings in their noses to discourage their activity. Cows could sometimes lift off rails with their horns and jump over low places, unless hampered by yokes made from forked limbs hung around their necks.

Leisure on a frontier farm was virtually unknown. When all other work was done, livestock required attention, and no excuse could save one from this labor. Even though grass might be bountiful, horses and cattle had to be driven to and from pasturage. Morning and night, cows had to be milked. This was sometimes the task of women, sometimes of boys, but always the cows inexorably claimed the morning and evening hours of somebody. Water had to be found for livestock, at either a stream, well, or spring. When watering troughs in winter froze solid, freshwater had to be drawn from a well or the ice broken in a nearby stream. Sheep were a difficult problem in many places because they had to be protected from wolves or dogs. Hogs were an everlasting nuisance, for when they ran wild to feed in the woods, they were not content with nature's provender but were constantly getting into cornfields and garden patches. A farmer was never free of the burden of looking after livestock.

The coming of cold weather meant hog-killing time, with additional work for everyone—men, women, and children. Fat porkers were rounded up, knocked on the head with an ax, and their throats cut. They were dipped in a barrel of boiling water to loosen bristles so they could be scraped clean. Then the white carcass was hung from a limb, gutted, and the edible parts (almost everything) saved. Liver, lungs (called lights), kidneys, and brains were highly prized. The small intestines were emptied, scraped, washed, and saved to be used for stuffed sausage. Some intestines were cleaned and eaten as chitterlings. Fat was placed in pots over a fire to try out (render) the lard. The residue from the fatty pieces, called cracklings, brown and almost dry, made shortening for cornbread. Lean trimmings were ground into sausage. Spareribs and backbone, regarded as especially tasty fresh meat, were eaten first. Shoulders, hams, and sides were put down in salt to season awhile before final curing in the smokehouse. All this preparation required immense labor, but a supply of pork products served as the main meat diet of most farm families, since far more pork was consumed than beef.

Not even the frontiersman's diversions were without effort and utilitarian purpose. His hunting and fishing helped supply his larder. When the weather was too cold for any useful labor on the farm, he could still take his rifle and go hunting for deer, bear, or small game. In regions near the salt licks in Kentucky, buffalo were numerous in the early days. And buffalo robes were warmer than blankets, as were bearskins. Not only did deer supply meat, but their hides also had many uses: material for jackets, trousers, leggings, moccasins, aprons, and strips of rawhide, which served wherever we today would use rope or twine. For a cap a frontiersman could find nothing more to his liking than a coonskin with the tail dangling to one side.

Trees were regarded as a hindrance, and nobody had yet thought of the conservation of timber. When a dry spell came and grass was scarce, farmers cut down trees with edible leaves and succulent twigs for the cattle to browse on. When a boy spied a vine heavy with grapes, entwined

A raccoon hunt. "When a hunter's dogs treed coon or possum, the easiest way to get the animal was to cut down the tree." From a wood engraving after W. T. Sheppard, in *Harper's Weekly* (September 21, 1867).

A wood sawyers' tournament in Indiana. From a wood engraving after a drawing by C. G. Bush, in *Harper's Weekly* (November 30, 1867).

high in a tree, he usually preferred to cut down the tree than to climb it. When a hunter's dogs treed coon or possum, the easiest way to get the animal was to cut down the tree. Bee trees, of course, also fell to the ax.

As neighborhoods developed, the social life of the community invariably served some useful purpose. House-raisings helped the new settler provide a quick shelter for his family. Contests in wood sawing and reaping helped develop skills and get a job done, as well as demonstrate the prowess of the local champions.

While the frontiersman and his sons were busy out of doors, his wife and daughters had their special work to do. Even so, they frequently lent a hand with hoe and ax when such labor was required. A frontier proverb said, "Man works from sun to sun, but woman's work is never done." She had the usual tasks of cooking the food over an open fire, but she also had to go to great labor to gather it. She searched the fields for greens in the spring and summer— edible plants that she boiled with a piece of bacon. Often the growing of garden truck, as well as gathering and pre-

69

A reaping match in Ohio. From a wood engraving by L. J. Bridgman, in A. Black, *The Story of Ohio* (1888).

paring the vegetables when they were ready to eat, was her particular duty.

Women also had to card, spin, and weave wool and flax into the cloth required for clothing; they then had to make the clothes. Only an occasional peddler came by the clearing with pieces of bright calico, pins, needles, and maybe a ribbon or two. From bits and pieces could be made the patchwork quilts dear to the hearts of pioneer America. Ornamental, as well as useful, the quilts provided a little color in a drab world and a means of self-expression in the endless variety of patterns that could be devised. Quilting bees, or parties, served as occasions for get-togethers for the women in the meager social life of the frontier.

Nearly everything worn by men, women, and children had to be fashioned at home from the elemental raw materials. For example, stockings had to be knit from wool that the women had previously spun into yarn. Sitting by a log fire in winter, her eyes heavy with sleep, the frontiersman's wife kept her knitting needles clicking until late into the night, for she had to see that everyone had socks and stockings. With all the heavy work that a woman had to perform, day in and day out, it is a marvel that she still had strength and courage to bear her children without medical doctor or hospital. If she was lucky, some neighbor woman with a knowledge of midwifery came to help. But many a frontier woman bore her child alone and did that which was necessary without the help of anyone.

The frontier woman had to know the rudiments of folk medicine, for she was called on to treat her children when they had ailments, and she was generally in demand for the sick on all occasions. She searched the fields for herbs believed beneficial. For example, cancerweed, beaten and made into a poultice, was believed useful in healing any open sore or boil. A hot poultice of onions applied to the chest was a remedy used for pneumonia and other congestions. Teas and infusions of many sorts were prescribed. Some women attained wide reputations for their curative lore and were much sought after in times of illness.

When death occurred, no undertaker came to attend to the last grim duties. The women of the family bathed the corpse, and it was laid out and dressed in the best clothes owned. The men made a rough coffin, dug the grave, and the burial was held more often than not without benefit of clergy. Someone spoke a stumbling prayer, someone

The peddler's wagon. Its occasional arrival brightened the day of women on the frontier. From a wood engraving after a drawing by C. G. Bush, in *Harper's Weekly* (June 20, 1868).

dropped wild flowers on the new made grave, and family and friends returned to the routine of life in the wilderness.

Always on the frontier danger lurked in many forms. Sudden and mysterious disease was a constant threat to life, to both old and young. Many children succumbed to measles, diphtheria, and other children's maladies. Typhoid fever and malaria were particular hazards that spared no age group. Many a man died of "cramp colic," probably appendicitis. Snakebites were common, and remedies varied: Some people held that the best cure was all the whiskey that the victim could absorb; others contended that a live chicken, split open and clapped upon the bitten spot, would draw out the poison. To prevent hydrophobia from the bite of a mad dog, certain stones, called madstones, were applied to the wound.

Most people believed implicitly in astrological lore, especially in the signs of the zodiac. Sick people were advised to avoid some medicines and some foods when the sign was in the head, or heart, or elsewhere. A cabin that had no other printed matter usually had a well-thumbed almanac that provided advice in these matters.

The almanac was also a guide to the planting of vegetables and field crops. Potatoes, turnips, and other root crops should be planted in the dark of the moon, though some farmers held that in their experience the light of the moon was best. Opinions varied, and long discussions about the best time of the moon for this and that occupied the attention of frontier folk.

Religion played an important part in the lives of frontier Kentuckians. Many of the settlers were Scotch Presbyterians, who in this period were profoundly influenced by several eloquent revivalist preachers. Revival services were held at camp meetings, sometimes under no other canopy than a brush arbor. Under the preachers' descriptions of the terrors of hell, the emotions of old and young frequently reached a crescendo that ended in convulsions, faintings, and other physical reactions. Certain preachers

72

Social life at a camp meeting, between services. From a print by Endicott after a painting owned by Joseph Smith, published for Smith (1838). *Courtesy, Library of Congress.*

also stirred factionalism until the Kentucky Presbyterians were divided into several dissenting sects, the most notable being that led by Thomas Campbell and his son, Alexander. The so-called Campbellites developed into the modern Disciples of Christ.

Members of other denominations, particularly Methodists and Baptists, were fairly numerous on the frontier. They, too, held camp meetings and revival services. In fact, frontiersmen of whatever sect or belief usually flocked to camp meetings regardless of denomination, for these services provided social contacts and human drama lacking in lives largely spent in isolation. Gradually the frontiersmen built churches which were supplied by itinerant or circuit-riding preachers.

The circuit riders distributed religious tracts and at times devoted some of their energy to teaching. When families were widely scattered in distant clearings, schools teaching even rudimentary subjects were few and far between, and such learning as children got came from their parents, the circuit rider, or some itinerant schoolmaster. As settlements grew thicker and the population increased, one-room schoolhouses were built and schoolmasters hired to teach the children within reach. Parents paid as best they could, sometimes in farm products, sometimes by providing room and board for the teacher. In Kentucky and western Pennsylvania occasionally both the preacher and the teacher received part of their pay in whiskey distilled from the

73

An itinerant schoolmaster. From *Harper's New Monthly Magazine* (May, 1872).

mash of Indian corn. Although no prejudice existed against either a parson's or a teacher's consuming part of this emolument, it represented a commodity both portable and potable to be used in barter, for much of local trade was carried on by barter.

In addition to an almanac, the only book in many a frontier cabin was the King James Version of the Bible. Frontier lawyers often learned quotations from the Bible that proved more useful before juries than legal precepts from Blackstone or other lawbooks.

The basis for rudimentary learning was the blue-back spelling book published in 1783 by Noah Webster of Connecticut. Eight years later, John Walker, an Englishman, brought out *A Critical Pronouncing Dictionary and Expositor of the English Language*, which competed with Webster's work and other American books. It was preferred by Virginians, many of whom had migrated to Kentucky, because it gave authority for pronunciations that they liked better than Webster's Connecticut speech.

Education was sketchy and elementary at best, but somehow frontiersmen managed to provide their children with a smattering of learning. Like their predecessors on the colonial frontiers, they were not willing to let their offspring "grow up barbarous in the wilderness"—not if they could help it. Some of the more uneducated settlers, of course, were content with such lore as they could learn from other woodsmen or from the Indians.

The opportunities—and the necessities—of frontier life produced a spirit of independence and self-reliance. Every individual knew that he had to shift for himself and make the best of any situation. Although frontiersmen gathered for house-raisings and other labor that required several men, they did not expect much help from anyone. In fact, so independent were the settlers in Kentucky that the Reverend Harry Toulmin, an English Unitarian minister who tried to encourage English emigration to Kentucky in 1793, declared that it was virtually impossible to hire any man to work for another.

"Shoemakers, tailors, smiths, carpenters, weavers, and most mechanics and husbandmen," Toulmin wrote, "are sure of employment . . . but the surest way is for a man to rent a few acres of land sufficient to maintain a few cows, hogs, and sheep so as not to be entirely dependent upon the exercise of their trade. Indeed few men will work for others as they soon become enabled either to rent or to purchase land." In further elaboration of this point, Toulmin commented: "It is peculiarly difficult for a man of property to hire a laborer. He must humor him a good deal and make him sit at the same table with him."[1]

Of the regions that attracted settlers just prior to the Revolution and immediately after, Kentucky aroused the greatest interest. In some degree this interest resulted from the promotion of land speculators like Richard Henderson and from tales circulated by and about Daniel Boone and other long hunters. Stories of the fertility of the bluegrass country, the abundance of game, and the fine forests (which indicated rich soil) circulated widely. Settlers swarmed into the country, chiefly from Virginia, North Carolina, and western Pennsylvania. So independent were they that they sometimes talked of setting up an independent country or of joining the Spaniards, who then controlled Louisiana. For fourteen years Virginia administered Kentucky as a county, but on June 1, 1792, Kentucky was admitted to the Federal Union, the second state to join the original thirteen, for Vermont had preceded it.

Kentucky pioneers set a sort of pattern in their modes of life, their behavior, and their attitudes for other pioneers who soon found their way westward, but regions differed markedly, depending on the origins of the majority of their new inhabitants. Many New Englanders, for example, took up land in Ohio and gave an air of New England to settlements north of the Ohio River, for they brought a distinct quality in their religion, social ideas, and educational aspirations. Ohio, for instance, established more schools and colleges than any of the other Midwestern states, largely as a result of the zeal of its New England settlers. But in the earliest stages most frontier regions repeated the experiences of preceding settlements, subject only to variations in terrain, climate, and problems with the aboriginal Indians.

4

The Lure of the Far-Distant West

IN THE last decade of the eighteenth century, pioneer farmers and traders were settling thickly along both the southern and the northern banks of the Ohio River. In 1790 Kentucky had 73,677 inhabitants; at least the United States' first census reported that number, though how many woodsmen escaped the count is anybody's guess. By 1800 Kentucky's population had grown to 220,955, and many of the settlers were beginning to complain that the country was crowded. A tradition reports that Daniel Boone regarded a neighbor nearer than 40 miles as too close. At any rate, pioneers were moving across the Ohio River and settling in Ohio, Indiana, and beyond. By 1800 Ohio had 45,365 new inhabitants, and Indiana numbered 5,641. Ten years later Kentucky's population had nearly doubled to 406,511, and Ohio's population had increased to 230,760. Like water spilling through a break in a dam, emigrants from the Eastern states were pouring westward.

The Ohio and Mississippi river systems offered an outlet for products of the farms and forests of this Western country. Flatboats loaded with corn, wheat, whiskey,

77

Jolly flatboat men. From an engraving by T. Doney after a painting by G. C. Bingham (1847). *Courtesy, Library of Congress.*

cured meat, deerskins, cowhides, and furs could be floated down the rivers to market in New Orleans. Ships from Europe swarmed into the Mississippi River port, and traders, eager for business, would buy almost any commodity produced by the upriver folk. Europe was greedy for agricultural products and furs. Since sugarcane was already supreme on the lower Mississippi, planters there also were eager to buy wheat, corn, and meat from the North.

The pioneer farmers and traders on both sides of the Ohio River were convinced that the prosperity of the West was assured. But one problem troubled them. New Orleans and the Mississippi River had to remain in friendly hands and be open to trade. If an unfriendly power shut the mouth of the Mississippi, Kentucky and Ohio would be ruined. Long mountain roads made access to Atlantic ports virtually impossible and certainly unprofitable.

From time to time the possibility of the closing of the Mississippi worried thoughtful folk. Since 1763, Spain had controlled the lower Mississippi and all Louisiana, which France had ceded to Spain to keep from surrendering it to England at the Peace of Paris. Eventually, France reasoned, she might get it back from Spain, but with England in possession of Louisiana, that vast territory, extending to the Rocky Mountains and the present borders of western Canada, would be lost forever. With the rise of Napoleon, France took steps to regain this prized territory and in October, 1800, made the secret Treaty of San Ildefonso reclaiming Louisiana. Since the treaty was secret and France was not taking immediate possession, Spain continued in command at New Orleans and at other garrison points along the Mississippi. For more than a decade before Napoleon forced Spain to return Louisiana, Spain had carried on intrigues with American politicians in the West in the hope of persuading the West to declare its independence of the young United States and align itself with Spain. Then New Orleans would be a free market for Western produce, the Mississippi would be permanently open to Western navigation, and the citizens of the Ohio and upper Mississippi valleys would have no worries about the permanence of their trade and prosperity.

A scoundrel named James Wilkinson, who wormed his way into the confidence of Washington, John Adams, and Jefferson, fostered these beliefs with hotheaded Kentuckians. That simultaneously he was carrying on intrigues with the British and French was indicative of his character. To frighten the Kentuckians and Ohioans, Spain from time to time closed the mouth of the Mississippi, though favored traders, Wilkinson among them, managed to get cargoes cleared. Because New England and the North generally believed that the West would eventually break away from the Federal Union anyway, politicians from that area were not eager to fight for the West's right of navigation on the Mississippi. Virginians and citizens of other Southern states, with greater interests in the West, were more concerned. The free navigation of the Mississippi, the allegiance to the United States of new territories in the West, and the eventual expansion of the United States beyond the Mississippi were problems confronting President Jefferson

79

when he got wind of the impending transfer of Louisiana to France. The prospect of Napoleon's ruling a vast realm bordering the Western frontier of the United States was not one to cheer a statesman, even one as optimistic as Jefferson.

Jefferson was keenly aware of the danger to the future development of the nation if a foreign power controlled the navigation of the Mississippi and its outlet to the sea. Deeply disturbed at the prospect that France would occupy New Orleans, Jefferson determined to attempt negotiations with Napoleon for its purchase. He had a trump card to play. Napoleon already had reason to fear that the British Navy might be powerful enough to nullify French influence in America. Jefferson planned to suggest to Napoleon that French possession of New Orleans and the mouth of the Mississippi would mean a union of British and United States maritime forces against France.

Accordingly, on April 18, 1802, Jefferson wrote to Robert Livingston, our minister in Paris, a letter whose substance he intended Livingston to transmit to Napoleon, along with an offer to buy New Orleans. In part, the letter read:

There is on the globe one single spot, the possessor of which is our natural and habitual enemy. It is New Orleans, through which the produce of three-eighths of our territory must pass to market, and from its [this territory's] fertility it will ere long yield more than half of our produce and contain more than half of our inhabitants. France, placing herself in that door, assumes to us the attitude of defiance. . . . The day that France takes possession of New Orleans . . . seals the union of two nations who in conjunction can maintain exclusive possession of the ocean. From that moment we must marry ourselves to the British fleet and nation.

Livingston transmitted his message and offer to buy New Orleans soon after the receipt of Jefferson's letter, but

Napoleon took no immediate notice of it. He was busy raising two armies—one to reconquer the island of Santo Domingo, where black slaves led by Toussaint L'Ouverture had rebelled against their French masters, and another to occupy Louisiana.

But fate intervened. The French army sent to Santo Domingo was destroyed by yellow fever and had to be reinforced with troops destined for Louisiana. That army in turn was decimated. After suffering this disaster, Napoleon turned his attention away from the New World and showed a sudden eagerness to get rid of a property that the British might take. In March, 1803, Jefferson sent James Monroe to Paris as special envoy to bargain for New Orleans and the surrounding territory. To the surprise of Monroe and Livingston, the French Minister of Foreign Affairs, Talleyrand, asked what they would give for the whole of Louisiana. After some haggling, the Americans agreed to pay 60,000,000 francs (about $12,000,000) and to assume any claims of its citizens against France. So for something less than $15,000,000 in totality, the United States acquired a territory that more than doubled the young nation's size and guaranteed its future expansion westward. Nobody knew the precise boundaries of the Louisiana Territory, but it extended from the Gulf of Mexico to Canada and westward to the Rocky Mountains. The boundaries between Louisiana and the Spanish possessions in the Southwest were also vague and ill-defined and would remain a matter of controversy. American jurisdiction over Florida would also have to wait for final settlement until 1821. But the Western destiny of the nation had been determined, and an enormous new realm now lay open to settlers. The nature of this region was still unknown and awaited the eyes of explorers.

Because France was in haste to sell Louisiana, and Jefferson, with farsighted intuition, was eager to buy, his commissioners, Monroe and Livingston, consummated the deal without further authorization. No cables or wireless in those days were available for quick communication. They dared not wait until sailing ships could transmit further written instructions, for Napoleon might change his mind.

From our point of vantage in time, we might think that all Americans would have rejoiced over the greatest real estate bargain in history. But such was not the case. Not everybody wanted to expand into the West; the New Englanders especially were opposed to Jefferson's plans.

The purchase of Louisiana was instantly condemned by a group who opposed Jefferson throughout his administration. The leaders of the Federalist Party—particularly Fisher Ames and Timothy Pickering of Massachusetts—were loudest in their condemnation of the President. The act deserved impeachment, they asserted, for the President had flouted the authority of Congress and had spent the people's money with reckless abandon for a useless wilderness. Timothy Dwight, president of Yale College—"Pope" Dwight, as he was called—attacked Jefferson on high moral grounds: The purchase of Louisiana was part of a plot to destroy religion in the United States!

Newspapers of 1803 pointed out the folly of wasting money, the danger of acquiring undefendable outposts, and the political trickery of the administration in adding radical citizens who would support Jeffersonian principles. In short, Louisiana would be the ruin of the country, and neither the lives nor property of honest citizens would henceforth be safe.

On August 2 the *New England Palladium*, the mouthpiece of Fisher Ames and his friends, printed a virulent editorial sarcastically ridiculing Jefferson's actions. "This purchase will cost each man in the United States who pays taxes more than *twenty dollars*," the newspaper cried. "Here is a map of the country painted red and yellow, extending to the Pacific Ocean, and including the dog-ribbed Indians. Here is a fine nursery for new States; new stars and satellites will move round the old Virginia orb. Members of Congress will come to Washington by way of

Cape Horn!" Surely only a half-crazy man like Jefferson could have hatched up such a scheme, the paper implied and continued its heavy sarcasm: "Here will be room enough for experiments upon man in all his varieties. But sober men, before they pay their twenty dollars, will ask if this world of wilderness is necessary or useful." Then, appealing to "men of goodsense," the *Palladium* asked: "Are we not already scattered over more land than we can cultivate, and have we not enough in a state of nature to resort to for ages? Does not this extension of limits enfeeble us, or will it not raise up independent and hostile neighbors? Is it not better to protect what we already possess, and secure our property at home, before we enter into speculations abroad?" Thus spoke the voice of "sensible men" who put their own little bailiwicks, with their immediate comforts and profits, ahead of the nation's good. To their own complete satisfaction they "proved" Jefferson not only a knave but also an ass.

On December 20 the *Palladium* reprinted an ironic editorial from a Maryland newspaper, the Fredericktown *Herald*, condemning Jefferson for organizing an army to take formal possession of Louisiana. Did we not buy the territory for a pretty penny? And did not the purchase ensure peaceable possession from the Spanish authorities (still residing in New Orleans despite Napoleon)? Or did it mean that perhaps the foolish Jefferson had been hoodwinked by the Frenchman, who had no real title to the territory? Perhaps Mr. Jefferson, in the same way, would buy from Napoleon the kingdom of China or the island of Great Britain? So the small men, the prudent, the careful men, who knew a thing or two about government, ridiculed the man in the Presidency who had looked beyond the nation's borders and had seen a vision of national greatness.

In the westward expansion of the United States, Fisher Ames—advocate of rule by "the wise, the good, and the rich"—foresaw disaster to the tight little commercial aristocracy that held control in New England. The new region was "foreign" and was peopled by radicals of every race and creed. Furthermore, the addition of Louisiana made the country too big. Even the original thirteen states were unmanageable. New England, on the other hand, was finite and comprehensible. Its ships might bring the riches of Europe and Asia to Salem and Boston; but it would never be contaminated by foreign contacts, and it would prudently manage to avoid troubles with great nations. Meanwhile, it would grow rich, its merchants would build fine houses, and some of the prosperity would dribble down to simpler folk, artisans and craftsmen, who would be brought up on the thrifty doctrines of "Pope" Dwight and the Congregational Church. Perhaps, if the country remained small, in time New England could induce the nation to follow its way. At least, New England could ensure its own prosperity. So reasoned Ames and the other conservatives of the Federalist Party. Jefferson, in buying Louisiana, had ruined everything. Disastrous contacts with "foreigners" and the incursion of radicals would make the New England dream unattainable. "As to the territory," Ames wrote on October 3, 1803, "the less of it the better. . . ."[1]

In 1811, when the question of the admission of the state of Louisiana was being debated in Congress, Josiah Quincy of Massachusetts gave utterance to the perennial fear of any relations with "foreigners." The question, he said, was whether the "proprietors of the good old United States shall manage their own affairs in their own way, or whether they and their Constitution and their political rights shall be trampled under foot by foreigners introduced through a breach of the Constitution." The framers of the Constitution, he insisted, would not have tolerated this invasion from beyond the Mississippi. "They were not madmen," Quincy cried hysterically. "They had not taken degrees in the hospital of idiocy. Why, sir, I have already heard of six states, and some say there will be, at no great distance of time, more." The "old" United States would be destroyed by the invaders from the West, Quincy asserted, as he reminded Congress that it would be responsible for delivering the nation into the hands of foreign radicals and infidels. "You have no authority," he shouted at Congress, "to throw the rights and liberties and property of this people into a hotch-potch of the wild men on the Missouri, nor with the mixed, though more respectable, race of Anglo-Hispano-Gallo-Americans who bask on the sands in the mouth of the Mississippi." If Louisiana should be admitted, he declared, the Union would be dissolved, and it was the duty of steady New England states to get ready for the separation, "amicably if they can, violently if they must."[2]

Long before the United States acquired Louisiana and before Thomas Jefferson became President, he had been interested in the exploration of the West beyond the Mississippi. While he was minister in Paris, Jefferson encountered an adventurer named John Ledyard who had been on Captain James Cook's last voyage to the Pacific and had seen the northwestern coast of America. Ledyard conceived the notion of going to Russia and of reaching the American coast from Siberia. He would then cross the continent on foot from west to east. In the winter of 1786, Jefferson tried through diplomatic channels to persuade the Russians to allow Ledyard to undertake this journey but failed. Nevertheless, Ledyard went to Russia on his own initiative and got into eastern Siberia before the Russian authorities changed their minds and sent him back via Poland.

Jefferson's next hope of trans-Mississippi exploration centered on a proposal that he put before the American Philosophical Society in 1792. Whatever Jefferson may have had in his mind, the avowed purpose of the plan was geographical exploration and scientific observation. A scientist, to "be attended by a single companion only, to avoid exciting alarm among the Indians," would make the journey, Jefferson stated. The scientist selected was a French

85

botanist, André Michaux, but the expedition collapsed, it is believed, because Jefferson probably decided that Michaux was more interested in spying for France than in furthering the interests of the United States, scientific or otherwise.

In the meantime, exploration of the Far West had received an unexpected stimulus from the discovery in 1792 of the mouth of a great river on the Northwest coast by Captain Robert Gray in the ship *Columbia*. He named the stream the Columbia River and claimed the territory for the United States. Gray was one of the ship captains engaged in the rapidly developing China trade, which depended for its prosperity on the collection of furs in the Northwest to be exchanged in Canton for Chinese products. The Chinese especially favored sea otter; but other furs were also in demand, and this trade, new to the Americans, proved extremely profitable. With a claim to a territory of unknown extent in the Northwest, with a great river that might lead deep into the American continent, perhaps with a short overland haul connecting with Eastern river systems, Jefferson and other like-thinking Americans dreamed of a water route across the continent that would tap sources of infinite wealth. They hoped that the Missouri or one of its tributaries would prove navigable to a point close to the Continental Divide. There they also hoped to find a navigable stream flowing west that would prove to be the Columbia or one of its tributaries.

Rumors of a great "River of the West" had been circulating for years. But nobody in the government had any certain knowledge of this river, nor had anyone even the vaguest notion of the height and expanse of the mountain ranges in the West. Until exploration proved that a water route to the Pacific was not feasible, planners in the capital of the United States would retain their hopes, as men since the seventeenth century had continued to believe that they might find a Northwest Passage to the Pacific by sea.

This dream of a water route to the Pacific was one of

Meriwether Lewis in frontier costume. From an engraving by Strickland after a water-color by C. de St. Memin, in *The Analectic Magazine* (May, 1816). Courtesy, Library of Congress.

many reasons that prompted Jefferson to send a message to Congress in January, 1803, asking for an appropriation to equip an expedition for the exploration of the trans-Mississippi West. Congress voted the funds, and Jefferson set about organizing what was to be the most famous overland journey in the history of the United States, the Lewis and Clark Expedition.

To be the leader, Jefferson chose his private secretary, Meriwether Lewis, a Virginian commissioned a captain in the United States Army. He allowed Lewis to choose a friend, William Clark, another Virginian, to be joint commander. For some curious reason, the War Department gave Clark a commission as second lieutenant in the artillery instead of a promised commission as captain, but he was called Captain Clark and was so designated in formal reports. Clark was a younger brother of George Rogers Clark, who had proved a hero in the war against the British and the Indians in the West during the Revolution.

Dual commands rarely are successful, but the arrangement between Lewis and Clark worked perfectly. Both were born leaders, who knew how to manage men and get the

William Clark. From a watercolor facsimile of the portrait by C. W. Peale. *Courtesy, Library of Congress.*

most out of them. Lewis had a keen scientific curiosity and possessed more book learning than Clark. But Clark was adept at handling boats, an excellent woodsman, and skillful in dealing with the Indians. For years afterward he was remembered by the Indians for his flaming hair and called the Red Head.

On June 20, 1803, President Jefferson signed detailed, written instructions, directed to Lewis, for the organization and direction of the expedition. At that time the President did not yet know the outcome of negotiations with the French. Not until about the first of July did the news reach Jefferson that his emissaries had purchased the whole of the Louisiana Territory and that his explorers would now be examining land belonging to the United States. That news created great excitement and gave added motivation to the expedition.

Jefferson hoped that Lewis and Clark could get the Indian tribes in the West to agree to peace pacts that would end intertribal wars. Negotiation with the Indians for the establishment of trading posts to compete with British traders from Canada was also one of the purposes that the leaders kept in mind. Undreamed developments in the future depended on the operation that President Jefferson entrusted to these two courageous Virginians.

The almost incredible success that they achieved was the result of careful, ingenious planning and intelligent discipline demanded by the leaders of their men. Preparations began in the summer of 1803 and continued through the summer and autumn. By December Lewis and Clark had picked a group of men and had decided on a campsite on the east bank of the Mississippi above St. Louis, where they would train and harden the men and complete preparations for a start west in the spring. They had planned to camp at La Charette on the Missouri, but the Spanish commandant, whom the French had left in charge, had not yet got the word that the Americans had bought Louisiana. Therefore, he prevented their move up the Missouri until he received official notification of the change.

The party for the entire journey included nine tough young Kentucky woodsmen, fourteen regulars from the United States Army who had volunteered for this duty, two French rivermen, a French interpreter and hunter whose name was anglicized to Drewyer, and a black servant of Clark's named York, who was to prove a marvel to the Indians along the way. From the men, the leaders chose

Captains Lewis and Clark holding a council with the Indians. From a woodcut in P. Gass, *A Journal of the Voyages and Travels of Capt. Lewis and Capt. Clarke* (1810 ed.).

three to serve as sergeants. Employed to go only as far as the Mandan Indian villages on the upper Missouri were a corporal and six soldiers, with nine boatmen to help with the transport of goods upstream. The initial party, therefore, consisted of forty-five men. Later in the Mandan country they hired a virtually worthless French interpreter named Toussaint Charbonneau because he could speak the language of the Minnetarees. But if Charbonneau proved a trifling, unreliable fellow, one of his two Indian wives, Sacajawea, a Shoshone, helped save the expedition from disaster when they encountered her people in the Rockies. As will be seen later, she deserves a place among the heroines of the American frontier. Of the men recruited and trained on the banks of the Mississippi in the winter of 1803–4 only one failed to survive the journey. He was Sergeant Charles Floyd, who died of what Clark put down in his badly spelled notes as a "Biliose Chorlick" (bilious colic), probably acute appendicitis.

For the journey up the Missouri, the party had a 55-foot-long keelboat propelled by a square sail and twenty-two oars, with covered decks fore and aft and covered, water-tight lockers between. In addition to the keelboat, the party also had two large pirogues—flatbottomed open boats with pointed bow and square stern—one rowed by six oars and the other by seven. Since the progress upstream would be slow, they took along two horses, which plodded along the riverbanks and kept up with the boats. These were to be used by the hunters in running down game needed for food.

Although they started with some food supplies, they expected to live off the country. Much of the cargo consisted of trading goods for the Indians: bright-colored cloth, blankets, coats, caps, and other articles of clothing that the Indians might want, hatchets, medals, beads, paints, trinkets, mirrors, and flags. The display of Indian goods must have made the keelboat look like a modern variety store when the crew was baling and packing the stuff. Much space was also required for guns, powder, and shot. The

Alluvial banks caving in along the Missouri River, 600 miles above St. Louis. From a painting (1832) in Catlin's Indian Gallery. *Courtesy, Smithsonian Institution.*

keelboat was armed with two small cannon, fore and aft, called swivel guns. So careful was the planning, that some of the gunpowder was sealed in watertight lead flasks. When the powder was used, the flasks were melted and molded into bullets.

After a winter of preparation and practice, the expedition got under way on Monday, May 14, 1804, with Clark in command because Lewis was detained for a week on official business and had to catch up with the party a week later. Their journey up the Missouri was slow and always dangerous. In many places, the banks had a habit of caving in as they approached, and at first the keelboat, heavily loaded at the stern, ran on submerged logs and snags. Mark Twain many years later in describing his own experiences as a Mississippi River pilot devoted some of his more pungent remarks to a description of the danger of the snags still persisting in the great river systems. Gradually Lewis and Clark learned the best method of navigation, and experience taught them how to pick safe places to tie up and camp.

Elk hunting from a canoe. From a Currier & Ives lithograph. Courtesy, Library of Congress.

Lewis, after joining the expedition, spent a great deal of time ashore riding or walking along the riverbanks, collecting botanical, mineral, and animal specimens that he thought worth preserving. He was the one with the greater scientific knowledge and interest. Clark managed the boats. The skills of the two leaders complemented each other in an effective way. Travel by water up the swift-flowing Missouri was slow; on some days they made only a few miles, but on good days they covered as much as 18 or 20 miles. Their progress was impeded by the snags, floating logs, sandbars, and caving banks.

Game was plentiful, and the party lived well on deer, elk, and bear, varied with duck, geese, and turkey. On August 23 they killed their first buffalo on the prairie a short distance above Elk Point, South Dakota. They salted down some of the meat for future use. From this point onward, they encountered buffalo frequently, and like many frontiersmen to follow them, they learned to value the buffalo as their best source of food.

As they proceeded up the Missouri, they observed Indians who watched them curiously but rarely appeared hostile. One of the objects of the expedition was to inform the Indians that the whole land now belonged to the Great Father in Washington and that it was his wish for them to live in peace with one another and with their white brothers. They were told that the Americans planned to establish trading posts, where they could sell their furs and buffalo robes and buy guns, powder, lead, blankets, cloth, tobacco, rum, and anything else that they might desire. Lewis and Clark distributed American flags, tobacco, medals, and trinkets to the chiefs and other Indians who seemed to deserve gifts.

Occasionally, however, Indians were unfriendly and threatening, but firmness on the part of the leaders and the obvious readiness of the men to defend themselves staved off attack. For example, on October 2, when the party reached the confluence of the Cheyenne River, above Pierre, South Dakota, they encountered hostile Yankton Indians, and Lewis noted in his journal that "we were in constant expectation of being attacked and were therefore forced to keep the party together and be on our guard." Under such circumstances they dared not send out a hunting party but depended on such game as came their way. Three days later Lewis remarked that "our game this day was a deer, a prairie wolf, and some goats [antelope] out of a flock that was swimming across the river." Although Indians from time to time threatened the party, they escaped serious trouble throughout the long journey to the Pacific Coast and back, and they never lost a man in any affray with the Indians.

The Americans were in constant touch with Indians all along their route. They did their best to impress on the natives the importance of keeping the peace so that they might profit from the trade that the Great Father in Washington was planning for them. Although Lewis and Clark managed to avoid overt trouble with any of the tribes along the Missouri, they ran the greatest risk with the tricky Sioux, particularly with a tribe of Sioux called Tetons in the neighborhood of the present city of Pierre. Having evaded the Tetons, the expedition pushed on to the country of the Mandans and prepared to establish winter quarters with this tribe near the modern site of Bismarck, North Dakota.

93

Stone with Horns—a chief of the Yankton Indians. From a portrait (1832) in Catlin's Indian Gallery. Courtesy, Smithsonian Institution.

On the way to the Mandans they had passed through encampments of Arikaras, who were at the time at war with the Mandans. The Arikaras, however, were friendly to the newcomers and happily traded them corn, beans, and pumpkins, which they raised in considerable quantities. The Arikara women were handsomer than the Sioux, Lewis commented, and were generous with their favors to the voyagers. York, the strong black servant of Captain Clark, was a particular favorite with the Indian women, said Lewis, for they "desired to preserve among them some memorial of this wonderful stranger." Everywhere York made a great hit with the Indians, who had never before seen a black man. His dancing and his feats of physical prowess especially impressed them.

By the first of November the expedition had reached the Mandan villages and had picked a wooded spot for their winter quarters. After a few busy days of felling cottonwood, elm, and ash trees, they erected a series of huts of four rooms each. Roofed with split logs and heavily banked with grass and clay, the houses were warm and snug against the arctic blasts of the Dakotan winter.

It was at this point, early in November, that Lewis and Clark, concerned about communicating with the Western Indians, hired as interpreter Charbonneau, who brought along his two wives, one being Sacajawea, who had a better knowledge of the Western Indian languages than her shiftless husband. She probably saved the expedition in the Rockies when she was able to persuade some of her tribesmen to sell horses and food to the explorers. Charbonneau proved less than useful and at times was a complete nuisance. So lazy that he shirked all the work he could avoid, he was constantly complaining and threatening to quit. From entries in his journal, Captain Clark clearly found it hard to put up with Charbonneau, but luckily he held his temper in check. In February, Sacajawea gave birth to a baby boy, who endured the rigors of the journey to the Pacific coast and the return.

War dance of the Teton Sioux. From a painting (1830's) in Catlin's Indian Gallery. Courtesy, *Smithsonian Institution.*

Fort Pierre and a Sioux village at the mouth of the Teton River, 1,200 miles above St. Louis. From a painting (1832) in Catlin's Indian Gallery. *Courtesy, Smithsonian Institution.*

Mandan village seen from a distance, 1,800 miles above St. Louis. From Catlin's Indian Gallery. *Courtesy, Smithsonian Institution.*

During the winter the men joined Indian hunting parties or hunted in groups of their own, and they sometimes came back with frostbitten feet and ears. The cold was intense. For instance, on December 8, a journal entry reported that Captain Lewis with fifteen men went out to hunt buffalo and brought back eight buffalo and one deer. But two men returned with badly frostbitten feet, for the cold "was so excessive that the air was filled with icy particles resembling a fog." Two days later Captain Clark took eighteen men and killed nine more buffalo, but "spent a cold, disagreeable night on the snow with no covering but a small blanket, sheltered by the hides of the buffalo they had killed." Skinning buffalo and cutting up the edible portions of the carcasses must have been miserable work in the bitter wind of the prairie. But nobody caught his death from exposure, and they managed to live in reasonable comfort until the ice broke up in the spring.

The explorers did their best to make friends with all the Indians who came to visit them while they were in winter quarters. The blacksmith gained great favor by making tools for the Indians out of any iron available and by sharpening their axes, knives, and spearpoints. Occasionally Lewis and Clark distributed a little rum and gave presents to visiting chiefs. Sometimes the men took part in Indian festivities in the Mandan villages and amused the Indians by their dancing. York was always a star performer. On March 9 a chief of the Minnetaree tribe came to

The interior of the hut of a Mandan chief. Bernard De Voto considered this picture by Bodmer "one of the best ever made of Indian life." From an aquatint in Wied-Neuwied, *Travels.*

Festivities in the Mandan village—the bull dance. From Catlin's Indian Gallery. *Courtesy, Smithsonian Institution.*

the camp and said he had heard that one man in the expedition was coal black. When York came forward, the chief, Lewis reported in his journal, could hardly believe his eyes but "spit on his finger and rubbed the skin in order to wash off the paint; nor was it until the Negro uncovered his head and showed his short hair that Le Borgne [the French name of this chief] could be persuaded that he was not a painted white man."

At last soft winds from the south brought a touch of warmth to the frozen prairie, and spring rains melted the snow and ice. The men had prepared for the time of departure by making dugout canoes out of cottonwood trees—frail craft for the rapids in the rivers ahead of them.

The keelboat, which was too heavy to go farther up the Missouri, was loaded with specimens, and the boatmen hired in St. Louis with two or three soldiers, making in all a crew of fifteen men, set sail for St. Louis. They carried letters and reports to President Jefferson. They arrived safely and sent both specimens and letters on to the President.

The remaining "permanent party," consisting now of thirty-two persons, set out on April 7 to make their way to the Pacific. They little knew what barriers lay ahead of them. In six makeshift canoes and two pirogues they hoped to reach the ocean.

As they proceeded westward, the country began to change from the flat prairie land to more rugged terrain. Animal life also changed. Though buffalo continued to be plentiful, they now began to see more elk and Rocky Mountain sheep. Bears and wolves were more numerous, and they made their first contacts with grizzlies. On May 5, Clark described one as a "verry large and a turrible looking animal, which we found verry hard to kill. We shot ten Balls into him before we killed him, & 5 of those Balls through his lights. This animal is the largest of the carnivorous kind I ever saw." As they were to learn, the grizzly

Captain Clark and his men shooting bears. From a woodcut in Gass, *Journal*.

was indeed a ferocious and dangerous beast, not to be wounded unless the hunter was certain of enough firepower to kill.

The canoes and pirogues often had to be towed along the banks by the men, using elkhide ropes, which stretched when wet and sometimes broke. At last when they reached a point on the river where the heavier pirogue could no longer be used, they dug a trench and buried it with some of their heaviest equipment, making what the French trappers called a *cache*, which the English pronounced "cash." They hoped to recover these supplies on their return.

On August 10 they reached a point at Red Rock River, southwest of Dillon, Montana, where Captain Lewis decided they would have to abandon hope of further water transportation until they could cross the mountains. They attached wheels, wooden circles sawed from the trunk of a 22-inch cottonwood tree, to some of their canoes and in this fashion hauled some of their supplies. The rest, which they could not carry or haul, they cached. Then began the long and difficult trek through the mountains by way of the Lemhi Pass, at a height of 8,000 feet. At this point they crossed the Continental Divide and began to look for the Columbia River, which they believed would take them to the sea. Unhappily, they had many rough miles and many hardships before they could float again on a river.

The cactus and the sharp volcanic rock in Idaho pierced their elkhide moccasins, long since substituted for the boots with which they began the journey. Their clothes were now made from deer and elkhides, and only their thick, long, uncut hair covered their heads. Game was now scarcer, and they had to eat some of the meat they had dried. Storms were frequent, with torrential rains, hail that bruised and bloodied their heads, and gales that sometimes nearly swept them off the trail. Most of the men suffered from stomach ailments, boils, and blisters. But morale remained high. At length they met Indians whom Sacajawea recognized as her own people, and from them they obtained

Fort Nez Perces. From a lithograph by Ford & West, in A. Ross, *Fur Hunters of the Far West* (1855).

twenty-nine horses to use as pack animals and for food if game failed them completely.

By the time they reached the country of the Nez Percé (pronounced nez purse) Indians they had acquired thirty-eight horses. It was now early October, and they had found navigable water again on the Clearwater River east of Lewiston, Idaho. After making new dugout canoes from pine trees in the vicinity, they once more began their journey by boat. They branded their horses and left them with the friendly Nez Percés, who promised to keep them until the explorers returned.

Following the Clearwater and the Snake, which had dangerous rapids requiring some portages, they reached the Columbia River on October 16. Forced to live on salmon, dried and fresh, the principal diet of the Indians, they were soon sick of the sight of fish. But game had disappeared. Occasionally they shot a few ducks and grouse. Having learned from the Indians that dogs were edible, they bought seven dogs and 20 pounds of dried horsemeat to vary their diet. Later they were glad to buy more dogs, which the men declared to be "sweet meat."

101

The journey down the Columbia, through rapids so dangerous that Clark ordered all the men who could not swim to walk on shore, required until November 19, when they reached the mouth of the river and saw the great rolling breakers of the Pacific Ocean. Their first camp was established on the north side of the river in what is now the state of Washington.

The welcome that the Pacific coast gave the first citizens of the United States to arrive overland was less than heart-warming. Rain fell in torrents; the days were cold and bleak; the food was unpalatable to men already surfeited on fish; and the Indians were dirty, thievish, and a nuisance. The explorers managed to buy a few of what Clark called "Wappato roots . . . equal to the Irish potato, . . . a tolerable substitute for bread." So far as they could tell, game was almost nonexistent in the neighborhood of their camp. The roar of the ocean bothered Clark, who said he saw no reason to call it Pacific. After a time the party established themselves on the south side of the river on a small rise in the swamp, built a stockade, and named it Fort Clatsop after the local Indians. Elk, they had heard, were plentiful on the Oregon side, and they needed the hides for clothing, as well as the meat for food. Jefferson had promised to send a ship with supplies for the return trip, but they looked in vain for the vessel that never came. They had to make do with such equipment as they had or could manufacture, and they had to prepare for the return in the spring and summer of 1806.

On Christmas Day, 1805, Clark wrote morosely in his journal that they would have spent the day feasting if they had had anything to eat. One of the sergeants lamented that they no longer had any "ardent spirits" with which to celebrate Christmas. Clark observed that they had nothing "either to raise our Sperits or even gratify our appetites. Our Diner concisted of pore Elk, so much Spoiled that we eate it thro mear necessity, Some pounded fish and a fiew roots." They could not even sleep in peace, for fleas in-

102

fested their damp blankets, and the sun shone so little that they could dry neither blankets nor clothing. Furthermore, their huts smoked abominably when they lit a fire. Altogether the American explorers spent a miserable Christmas and thought gloomily of the winter months ahead. They would be glad to set out again on the return, even if no ship came to relieve their needs.

The tedious winter, dreary and wet, finally drew to a close. The long gray days had not been entirely wasted. Lewis and Clark got into shape notes about the outward journey, they studied the terrain, and they analyzed the opportunities for trade on that coast. Buying a few sea otter skins from the Indians, they investigated the potentialities of trade in sea otter furs. They also picked up news of traders who had already touched on the Northwest coast. A little later Lewis and Clark's information would stir John Jacob Astor to send out two expeditions, one by sea in 1810 and another overland in 1811, to establish a trading post, called Astoria, at the mouth of the Columbia River. The threat of attack by sea during the War of 1812 induced Astor, however, to sell out to his British rivals, the North West Company. Nevertheless, data collected by Lewis and Clark in time led to the development of a flourishing American trade in furs.

When spring, still rainy and wet, finally came to the Pacific coast, the explorers were eager to pack up and be off on their long journey back across the continent. After another heavy downpour of rain on March 23, 1806, the sun burst from behind a cloud, and the expedition broke camp about noon. They shook the mud of Fort Clatsop from their moccasins, beat the fleas out of their blankets, packed their belongings into canoes, and started the backbreaking journey against the current up the swift-flowing Columbia. They were not sorry to leave Fort Clatsop, whatever the future might hold for them. But Clark noted rather philosophically in his journal on the day of their departure that they had "lived as well as we had any right to expect, . . . never one day without 3 meals of some kind a day, either pore Elk meat or roots, nothwithstanding the repeated fall of rain, which has fallen almost constantly. . . ."

Slowly they made their way up the Columbia and overland into the Rockies. Game was scarce. The salmon had not yet begun to run, and even the Indians along the rivers were hungry. As a precaution against starvation, the party traded with the Indians for such roots and dried meat as they could get. One expedient was to round up as many Indian dogs as they could find. Dogmeat was better than no meat. Clark on April 28 reported that one of the men, sent out "to lay in as maney fat dogs as he could procure, . . . obtained 10." Before long they had another string of dogs, and they acquired a few horses fat enough to slaughter. In some fashion they would stay alive until they reached the country of buffalo, deer, and bear, where they knew they again could eat well.

On the return journey Clark followed the Yellowstone River to the Missouri, but Lewis, with nine men, took a more northerly route to the Great Falls of the Missouri, for he wanted to explore the Marias River to the north, which he had reached on the outward journey. Lewis and his men encountered hostile Blackfoot Indians and, in a fight, killed two of them. During the entire journey, outward and back, this was the only encounter that resulted in the killing of Indians by men of the expedition. Lewis and his group left the scene as fast as their horses could carry them to avoid further trouble with this tribe, but the enmity that the killings precipitated lasted for years to come.

Lewis and his party having made a rendezvous with the main group under Clark on the Missouri below the mouth of the Yellowstone, the expedition now made rapid progress downstream in their canoes. At the Mandan villages they left Charbonneau, Sacajawea, and their boy, a stout youngster whom Clark had named Pompey. The rugged redheaded captain had grown fond of the child, and he wrote

Stu-mick-o-sucks—the Buffalo Bull's Back Fat, head chief of the Blackfoot tribe. From the portrait by Catlin (1832) in his Indian Gallery. *Courtesy, Smithsonian Institution.*

in his journal on August 17: "I offered to take his little son, a butifull promising child who is 19 months old to which they both, himself and wife, wer willing provided the child had been weened. They observed that in one year the boy would be sufficiently old to leave his mother & he would then take him to me if I would be so friendly as to raise the child for him in such manner as I thought proper, to which I agreed." And that is what Clark actually did. But Pompey's career is the theme for another story.

As the explorers got farther down the Missouri, they began to meet trappers and traders heading upstream. Already news of beaver, buffalo, and bear had excited adventurous souls ready to risk life and limb on the far frontiers. From one trader on September 6 they obtained a gallon of whiskey, and Clark duly noted that they "gave to each man of the party a dram, which is the first spiritious licquor which had been tasted by any of them since the 4 of July 1805." From other traders they managed to replenish their supply of tobacco, a great relief to men who had been forced to chew the inner bark of willow trees in lieu of anything better. On September 14 they met a friendly boatman headed upstream, who gave them biscuit, pork, and onions and more whiskey so that Clark reported that "our party received a dram and Snug Songs untill 11 oClock at night in the greatest harmoney."

Clearly life was becoming more bearable as the great journey drew to a close. About noon on September 23, 1806, the expedition tied up its canoes at St. Louis. The two leaders hastened to get off letters to President Jefferson, who, like everyone else, had given them up for lost. The little town of St. Louis outdid itself in hospitality, to both the leaders and the men. Every man was a hero, for no expedition had yet performed such miracles of endurance or ended so successfully. Although Lewis and Clark had not found the hoped-for water route to the Pacific, they had explored the extremities of the Louisiana Territory, plunged beyond into the unknown West, and opened the way for further exploration that would occupy the interest and attention of Americans for the next fifty years. They were the forerunners of numbers of frontiersmen, trappers, hunters, and mountain men in search of beaver who in the next few decades would infiltrate this wild and hitherto unknown country.

One man of the party, John Colter, did not come back to St. Louis. Two trappers with whom Colter talked at the Mandan villages persuaded him to join them in a search for beaver. They had traps, equipment, and supplies and offered to make Colter a third sharer in whatever they caught. After consultation, the leaders decided that Colter might leave the expedition if all the rest of the group promised to go on to St. Louis. That was agreed, and Colter stayed. With no companion, he made a long journey through what is now Yellowstone Park and discovered the hot springs, geysers, rumbling mountains, and other wonders of that extraordinary region.

To reward Lewis, President Jefferson in 1807 made him governor of the Louisiana Territory. In October, 1809, he had to go to Washington to consult with government authorities about affairs in Louisiana. On the way, following the Natchez Trace, a military road cut through the wilderness from Nashville, Tennessee, to Natchez, Mississippi, his party lost two horses. Leaving his companions to look for the horses, Lewis pushed ahead, promising to wait at the first white habitation. Stopping for the night at a country tavern run by a man and his wife named Grinder, about 60 miles southwest of Nashville, Lewis was either murdered or committed suicide. His death to this day remains a mystery, but evidence points to foul play. The state of Tennessee later erected near the spot a monument to the memory of a man regarded as an adopted citizen of Tennessee. Thus ended the career of a brilliant and courageous explorer.

About the time that Lewis was appointed governor of the Louisiana Territory, Clark was made superintendent of Indian Affairs, with headquarters in St. Louis. His skill in dealing with the Indians and his honesty and integrity brought honor to the office. From 1813 to 1821 he was governor of the Missouri Territory, carved out of a portion of the original Louisiana Purchase. During the War of 1812 he performed valiant service against the British and their Indian allies, and later he negotiated important treaties with the Indians. From 1821 until his death in 1838 he was again the able and effective superintendent of Indian Affairs.

The explorations of Lewis and Clark were the prelude to many other expeditions designed to reveal the nature of the Western country. Even while Lewis and Clark were making their overland journey to the Pacific, a young Army lieutenant, Zebulon Pike, led a party northward in an effort to discover the headwaters of the Mississippi River. In 1806–7, Pike led another expedition into the Southwest and explored Colorado and the region beyond. Pikes Peak, which he did not succeed in climbing, is named after him. Having gone beyond the Louisiana Purchase into Spanish territory, he and his men were taken captive by the Spaniards, who eventually marched them back across the border.

From this time on, Americans were continually probing the Western country trying to find easy passages across the mountains; they brought back information useful to adventurous souls who wished to trade with the Indians, hunt buffalo, or, in the end, move West as settlers. Some of the most helpful guides to the early Western travelers were the so-called mountain men, daring trappers who took their lives in their hands to seek beaver pelts in the Rocky Mountains. They discovered trails and passes over which they later led other adventurers in the West.

Daily Life on the St. Louis Frontier (1846): A Description by Francis Parkman

In the spring of 1846, Francis Parkman, a rather frail young man from Boston, two years out of Harvard, with a companion, Quincy Adams Shaw, went to St. Louis to start on a summer adventure that Parkman later described in *The Oregon Trail*. First published in the *Knickerbocker Magazine*, beginning in 1847, it had many editions. St. Louis was the point of departure for the distant West, and there Parkman and his companion outfitted themselves for a trip that took them through Missouri, Kansas, Nebraska, Wyoming, and Colorado. The following descriptions of the life encountered in St. Louis, Independence, and Westport (the present site of Kansas City), Fort Laramie, and Bent's Fort are excerpts from one of the most popular narratives of early adventure in the Wild West.

Last spring, 1846, was a busy season in the city of St. Louis. Not only were emigrants from every part of the country preparing for the journey to Oregon and California, but an unusual number of traders were making ready their wagons and outfits for Santa Fe. The hotels were crowded, and the gunsmiths and saddlers were kept constantly at work in providing arms and equipments for the different parties of travellers. Steamboats were leaving the levee and passing up the Missouri, crowded with passengers on their way to the frontier.

In one of these, the *Radnor*, since snagged and lost, my friend and relative, Quincy Adams Shaw, and myself, left St. Louis on the 28th of April, on a tour of curiosity and amusement to the Rocky Mountains. The boat was loaded until the water broke alternately over her guards. Her upper deck was covered with large wagons of a peculiar form, for the Santa Fe trade, and her hold was crammed with goods for the same destination. There were also the equipments and provisions of a party of Oregon emigrants, a band of mules and horses, piles of saddles and harness, and a multitude of nondescript articles, indispensable on the prairies. Almost hidden in this medley was a small French cart, of the sort very appropriately called a "mule killer," beyond the frontiers, and not far distant a tent, together with a miscellaneous assortment of boxes and barrels. The whole equipage was far from prepossessing in its appearance; yet, such as it was, it was destined to a long and arduous journey on which the persevering reader will accompany it.

The passengers on board the *Radnor* corresponded with her freight. In her cabin were Santa Fe traders, gamblers, speculators, and adventurers of various descriptions, and her steerage was crowded with Oregon emigrants, "mountain men," negroes, and a party of Kanzas [*sic*] Indians, who had been on a visit to St. Louis.

Thus laden, the boat struggled upward for seven or eight days against the rapid current of the Missouri, grating upon snags and hanging for two or three hours at a time upon sandbars. We entered the mouth of the Missouri in a drizzling rain, but the weather soon became clear, and showed distinctly the broad and turbid river, with its eddies, its sandbars, its ragged islands and forest covered shores. The Missouri is constantly changing its course; wearing away its banks on one side, while it forms new ones on the other. Its channel is continually shifting. Islands are formed, and then washed away, and while the old forests on one side are undermined and swept off, a young growth springs up from the new soil upon the other. With all these changes, the water is so charged with mud and sand that, in spring, it is perfectly opaque, and in a few minutes deposits a sediment an inch thick in the bottom of a tumbler. The river was now high; but when we descended in the autumn it was fallen very low, and all the secrets of its treacherous shallows were exposed to view. It was frightful to see the dead and broken trees, thickset as a military abattis, firmly imbedded in the sand, and all pointing downstream, ready to impale any unhappy steamboat that at high water should pass over them.

In five or six days we began to see signs of the great western movement that was taking place. Parties of emigrants, with their tents and wagons, were encamped on open spots near the bank, on their way to the common rendezvous at Independence. On a rainy day, near sunset, we reached the landing of this place, which is some miles from the river, on the extreme frontier of Missouri. The scene was characteristic, for here were represented at one view the most remarkable features of this wild and enterprising region. On the muddy shore stood some thirty or forty dark slavish-looking Spaniards, gazing stupidly out from beneath their broad hats. They were attached to one of the Santa Fe companies, whose wagons were crowded together on the banks above. In the midst of these, crouching over a smoldering fire, was a group of Indians, belonging to a remote Mexican tribe. One or two French hunters from the mountains, with their long hair and buckskin dresses, were looking at the boat; and seated on a log close at hand were three men, with rifles lying across their knees. The foremost of these, a tall, strong figure, with a clear blue eye and an open, intelligent face, might very well represent that race of restless and intrepid pioneers whose axes and rifles have opened a path from the Alleghenies to the western prairies. He was on his way to Oregon, probably a more congenial field to him than any that now remained on this side of the great plains.

Early on the next morning we reached Kanzas [sic] about five hundred miles from the mouth of the Missouri. Here we landed, and leaving our equipments in charge of Colonel Chick, whose log house was the substitute for a tavern, we set out in a wagon for Westport, where we hoped to procure mules and horses for the journey.

It was a remarkably fresh and beautiful May morning. The woods, through which the miserable road conducted us, were lighted by the bright sunshine and enlivened by a multitude of birds. We overtook on the way our late fellow travelers, the Kanzas Indians, who, adorned with all their finery, were proceeding homeward at a round pace; and whatever they might have seemed on board the boat, they made a very striking and picturesque feature in the forest landscape.

Westport was full of Indians, whose little shaggy ponies were tied by dozens along the houses and fences. Sacs and Foxes, with shaved heads and painted faces, Shawanoes and Delawares, fluttering in calico frocks and turbans, Wyandots dressed like white men, and a few wretched Kanzas wrapped in old blankets, were strolling about the streets, or lounging in and out of the shops and houses.

As I stood at the door of the tavern, I saw a remarkable-looking personage coming up the street. He had a ruddy face, garnished with the stumps of a bristly red beard and moustache; on one side of his head was a round cap with a knob at the top, such as Scottish laborers sometimes wear; his coat was of a nondescript form, and made of a gray Scotch plaid, with the fringes hanging all about it; he wore trousers of coarse homespun, and hob-nailed shoes; and to complete his equipment, a little black pipe was stuck in one corner of his mouth. In this curious attire, I recognized Captain C——, of the British army, who, with his brother, and Mr. R——, an English gentleman, was bound on a hunting expedition across the continent. I had seen the captain and his companions at St. Louis. They had now been for some time at Westport, making preparations for their departure, and waiting for a reinforcement, since they were too few in number to attempt it alone. They might, it is true, have joined some of the parties of emigrants who were on the point of setting out for Oregon and California; but they professed great disinclination to have any connection with the "Kentucky fellows."

The captain now urged it upon us, that we should join

111

forces and proceed to the mountains in company. Feeling no greater partiality for the society of the emigrants than they did, we thought the arrangement a good one, and consented to it. Our future fellow travelers had installed themselves in a little log house, where we found them surrounded by saddles, harness, guns, pistols, telescopes, knives, and in short their complete appointments for the prairie. R——, who had a taste for natural history, sat at a table stuffing a woodpecker; the brother of the captain, who was an Irishman, was splicing a trail rope on the floor. The captain pointed out, with much complacency, the different articles of their outfit. "You see," said he, "that we are all old travelers. I am convinced that no party ever went upon the prairie better provided." The hunter whom they had employed, a surly-looking Canadian, named Sorel, and their muleteer, an American ruffian from St. Louis, were lounging about the building. In a little log stable close at hand were their horses and mules, selected with excellent judgment by the captain.

We left them to complete their arrangements, while we pushed our own to all convenient speed. The emigrants, for whom our friends professed such contempt, were encamped on the prairie about eight or ten miles distant, to the number of a thousand or more, and new parties were constantly passing out from Independence to join them. They were in great confusion, holding meetings, passing resolutions, and drawing up regulations, but unable to unite in the choice of leaders to conduct them across the prairie. Being at leisure one day, I rode over to Independence. The town was crowded. A multitude of shops had sprung up to furnish the emigrants and Santa Fe traders with necessaries for their journey; and there was an incessant hammering and banging from a dozen blacksmiths' sheds, where the heavy wagons were being repaired, and the horses and oxen shod. The streets were thronged with men, horses, and mules. While I was in the town, a train of emigrant wagons from Illinois passed through, to join the camp on the prairie, and stopped in the principal street. A multitude of healthy children's faces were peeping out from under the covers of the wagons. Here and there a buxom damsel was seated on horseback, holding over her sunburnt face an old umbrella or a parasol, once gaudy enough, but now miserably faded. The men, very sober-looking country-men, stood about their oxen; and as I passed I noticed three old fellows, who, with their long whips in their hands, were zealously discussing the doctrine of regeneration. The emigrants, however, are not all of this stamp. Among them are some of the vilest outcasts in the country. I have often perplexed myself to divine the various motives that give impulse to this migration; but whatever they may be, whether an insane hope of a better condition in life, or a desire of shaking off restraints of law and society, or mere restlessness, certain it is, that multitudes bitterly repent the journey, and, after they have reached the land of promise, are happy enough to escape from it.

In the course of seven or eight days we had brought our preparations nearly to a close. . . . [Reports on a terrific rainstorm.]

We ourselves had our share of the deluge. . . . We were leading a pair of mules to Kanzas when the storm broke. Such sharp and incessant flashes of lightning, such stunning and continuous thunder I had never known before. The woods were completely obscured by the diagonal sheets of rain that fell with a heavy roar, and rose in spray from the ground, and the streams swelled so rapidly that we could hardly ford them. At length, looming through the rain, we saw the log house of Colonel Chick, who received us with his usual bland hospitality; while his wife, who, though a little soured and stiffened by a long course of camp meet-ings, was not behind him in goodwill, supplied us with the means of bettering our drenched and bedraggled condition. The storm clearing away at about sunset opened a noble prospect from the porch of the colonel's house which stands upon a high hill. The sun streamed from the breaking clouds upon the swift and angry Missouri, and on the vast expanse of forest that stretched from its banks back to the distant bluffs. . . .

Accordingly, our preparation being now complete, we

113

attempted one fine morning to begin our journey. The first step was an unfortunate one. No sooner were our animals put in harness than the shaft mule reared and plunged, burst ropes and straps, and nearly flung the cart into the Missouri. Finding her wholly uncontrollable, we exchanged her for another, with which we were furnished by our friend Mr. Boone, of Westport, a grandson of Daniel Boone, the pioneer. This foretaste of prairie experience was very soon followed by another. Westport was scarcely out of sight when we encountered a deep muddy gully, of a species that afterward became but too familiar to us, and here for the space of an hour or more the cart stuck fast.

Emerging from the mudholes of Westport, we pursued our way for some time along the narrow track, in the checkered sunshine and shadow of the woods, till at length, issuing into the broad light, we left behind us the farthest outskirts of the great forest, that once spread from the western plains to the shore of the Atlantic. Looking over an intervening belt of bushes, we saw the green, oceanlike expanse of prairie, stretching swell beyond swell to the horizon.

It was a mild, calm spring day; a day when one is more disposed to musing and reverie than to action, and the softest part of his nature is apt to gain the upper hand. I rode in advance of the party, as we passed through the bushes, and, as a nook of green grass offered a strong temptation, I dismounted and lay down there. All the trees and saplings were in flower, or budding into fresh leaf; the red clusters of the maple blossoms and the rich flowers of the Indian apple were there in profusion; and I was half inclined to regret leaving behind the land of gardens, for the rude and stern scenes of the prairie and the mountains.

Meanwhile the party came in sight out of the bushes. Foremost rode Henry Chatillon, our guide and hunter, a fine athletic figure, mounted on a hardy gray Wyandot pony. He wore a white blanket coat, a broad hat of felt, moccasins, and trousers of deerskin, ornamented along the seams with rows of long fringes. His knife was stuck in his belt; his bullet pouch and powder horn hung at his side, and his rifle lay before him resting against the high pommel of his saddle, which, like all his equipments, had seen hard service, and was much the worse for wear.

Shaw followed close, mounted on a little sorrel horse, and leading a larger animal by a rope. His outfit, which resembled mine, had been provided with a view to use rather than ornament. It consisted of a plain, black Spanish saddle, with holsters of heavy pistols, a blanket rolled up behind, and the trail rope attached to his horse's neck hanging coiled in front. He carried a double-barreled smoothbore, while I had a rifle of some fifteen pounds weight. At that time our attire, though far from elegant, bore some marks of civilization, and offered a very favorable contrast to the inimitable shabbiness of our appearance on the return journey. A red flannel shirt, belted around the waist like a frock, then constituted our upper garment; moccasins had supplanted our failing boots; and the remaining essential portion of our attire consisted of an extraordinary article, manufactured by a squaw out of smoked buckskin.

Our muleteer, Deslauriers, brought up the rear with his cart, wading ankle-deep in the mud, alternately puffing at his pipe, and ejaculating in his prairie patois, *"Sacré enfant de garce!"* as one of the mules would seem to recoil before some abyss of unusual profundity. The cart was of the kind that one may see by scores around the marketplace at Quebec, and had a white covering to protect the articles within. These were our provisions and a tent, with ammunition, blankets, and presents for the Indians.

We were in all four men with eight animals; for besides the spare horses led by Shaw and myself, an additional mule was driven along with us as a reserve in case of accident.

After this summing up of our forces, it may not be amiss to glance at the characters of the two men who accompanied us.

Deslauriers was a Canadian, with all the characteristics of the true Jean Baptiste. Neither fatigue, exposure, nor hard labor could ever impair his cheerfulness and gaiety, or his politeness to his *bourgeois;* and when night came, he would sit down by the fire, smoke his pipe, and tell stories with the utmost contentment. The prairie was his element. Henry Chatillon was of a different stamp. When we were at St. Louis, several gentlemen of the Fur Company had kindly offered to procure for us a hunter and guide suited for our purposes, and on coming one afternoon to the office, we found there a tall and exceedingly well-dressed man, with a face so open and frank that it attracted our notice at once. We were surprised at being told that it was he who wished to guide us to the mountains. He was born in a little French town near St. Louis, and from the age of fifteen years had been constantly in the neighborhood of the Rocky Mountains, employed for the most part by the company, to supply their forts with buffalo meat.

As a hunter, he had but one rival in the whole region, a man named Simoneau, with whom, to the honor of both of them, he was on terms of the closest friendship. He had arrived at St. Louis the day before, from the mountains, where he had been for four years; and he now asked only to go and spend a day with his mother, before setting out on another expedition. His age was about thirty; he was six feet high, and very powerfully and gracefully molded. The prairies had been his school; he could neither read nor write, but he had a natural refinement and delicacy of mind, such as is rare even in women. His manly face was a mirror of uprightness, simplicity, and kindness of heart; he had, moreover, a keen perception of character, and a tact that would preserve him from flagrant error in any society.

Henry had not the restless energy of an Anglo-American. He was content to take things as he found them; and his chief fault arose from an excess of easy generosity, not conducive to thriving in the world. Yet it was commonly remarked of him, that whatever he might choose to do with what belonged to himself, the property of others was always safe in his hands. His bravery was as much celebrated in the mountains as his skill in hunting; but it is characteristic of him that in a country where the rifle is the chief arbiter between man and man, he was very seldom involved in quarrels. Once or twice, indeed, his quiet good nature had been mistaken and presumed upon, but the consequences of the error were such, that no one was ever known to repeat it. No better evidence of the intrepidity of his temper could be asked, than the common report that he had killed more than thirty grizzly bears. He was a proof of what unaided nature will sometimes do. I have never, in the city or in the wilderness, met a better man than my true-hearted friend, Henry Chatillon. . . .

We were soon free of the woods and bushes, and fairly upon the broad prairie. Now and then a Shawanoe passed us, riding his little shaggy pony at a "lope"; his calico shirt, his gaudy sash, and the gay handkerchief bound around his snaky hair, fluttering in the wind. At noon we stopped to rest not far from a little creek, replete with frogs and young turtles. There had been an Indian encampment at the place, and the framework of the lodges still remained, enabling us very easily to gain a shelter from the sun, by merely spreading one or two blankets over them. Thus shaded, we sat upon our saddles, and Shaw for the first time lighted his favorite Indian pipe; while Deslauriers was squatted over a hot bed of coals, shading his eyes with one hand, and holding a little stick in the other, with which he regulated the hissing contents of the frying pan. The horses were turned to feed among the scattered bushes of a low oozy meadow. A drowsy spring-like sultriness pervaded the air, and the voices of ten thousand young frogs and insects, just awakened into life, rose in varied chorus from the creek and the meadows. . . .

[Early in the summer Parkman and his party reached Fort Laramie. He describes life at this frontier outpost.]

Looking back, after the expiration of a year, upon Fort Laramie and its inmates, they seem less like a reality than like some fanciful picture of the olden time; so different was the scene from any which this tamer side of the world can present. Tall Indians, enveloped in their white buffalo robes, were striding across the area or reclining at full length on the low roofs of the buildings which enclosed it. Numerous squaws, gayly bedizened, sat grouped in front of the rooms they occupied; their mongrel offspring, restless

117

and vociferous, rambled in every direction through the fort; and the trappers, traders, and *engagés* of the establishment were busy at their labor or their amusements.

We were met at the gate, but by no means cordially welcomed. Indeed, we seemed objects of some distrust and suspicion, until Henry Chatillon explained that we were not traders, and we, in confirmation, handed to the *bourgeois* [trader in charge] a letter of introduction from his principals. He took it, turned it upside down, and tried hard to read it; but his literary attainments not being adequate to the task, he applied for relief to the clerk, a sleek, smiling Frenchman, named Monthalon. The letter read, Bordeaux (the *bourgeois*) seemed gradually to awaken to a sense of what was expected of him. Though not deficient in hospitable intentions, he was wholly unaccustomed to act as master of ceremonies. Discarding all formalities of reception, he did not honor us with a single word, but walked swiftly across the area, while we followed in some admiration to a railing and a flight of steps opposite the entrance. He signed to us that we had better fasten our horses to the railing; then he walked up the steps, tramped along a rude balcony, and kicking open a door, displayed a large room, rather more elaborately furnished than a barn. For furniture it had a rough bedstead, but no bed; two chairs, a chest of drawers, a tin pail to hold water, and a board to cut tobacco upon. A brass crucifix hung on the wall, and close at hand a recent scalp, with hair full a yard long, was suspended from a nail. . . .

This apartment, the best in Fort Laramie, was that usually occupied by the legitimate *bourgeois*, Papin, in whose absence the command devolved upon Bordeaux. The latter, a stout, bluff little fellow, much inflated by a sense of his new authority, began to roar for buffalo robes. These being brought and spread upon the floor, formed our beds; much better ones than we had of late been accustomed to. Our arrangements made, we stepped out to the balcony to take a more leisurely survey of the long looked-for haven at which we had arrived at last. Beneath us was the square area surrounded by little rooms, or rather cells, which opened upon it. These were devoted to various purposes,

118

but served chiefly for the accommodation of the men employed at the fort, or of the equally numerous squaws whom they were allowed to maintain in it. Opposite to us rose the blockhouse above the gateway; it was adorned with the figure of a horse at full speed, daubed upon the boards with red paint, and exhibiting a degree of skill which might rival that displayed by the Indians in executing similar designs upon their robes and lodges. A busy scene was enacting in the area. The wagons of Vaskiss, an old trader, were about to set out for a remote post in the mountains, and the Canadians were going through their preparations with all possible bustle, while here and there an Indian stood looking on with imperturbable gravity.

Fort Laramie is one of the posts established by the "American Fur Company," which well-nigh monopolizes the Indian trade of this region. Here its officials rule with an absolute sway; the arm of the United States has little force; for when we were there, the extreme outposts of her troops were about seven hundred miles to the eastward. The little fort is built of bricks dried in the sun, and externally is of an oblong form, with bastions of clay, in the form of ordinary blockhouses, at two of the corners. The walls are about fifteen feet high, and surmounted by a slender palisade. The roofs of the apartments within, which are built close against the walls, serve the purpose of a banquette.

Within, the fort is divided by a partition: on one side is the square area, surrounded by the storerooms, offices, and apartment of the inmates; on the other is the *corral*, a narrow place, encompassed by the high clay walls, where at night, or in presence of dangerous Indians, the horses and mules of the fort are crowded for safekeeping. The main entrance has two gates, with an arched passage intervening. A little square window, high above the ground, opens laterally from an adjoining chamber into this passage; so that when the inner gate is closed and barred, a person without may still hold communication with those within, through this narrow aperture. This obviates the necessity of admitting suspicious Indians, for purposes of trading, into the body of the fort; for when danger is apprehended, the inner gate is shut fast, and all traffic is carried on by means of the window. . . .

[Describes visit of Indians.]

The discordant jingling of a bell, rung by a Canadian in the area, summoned us to supper. The repast was served on a rough table in one of the lower apartments of the fort, and consisted of cakes of bread and dried buffalo meat—an excellent thing for strengthening the teeth. At this meal were seated the *bourgeois* and superior dignitaries of the establishment, among whom Henry Chatillon was worthily included. No sooner was it finished than the table was spread a second time (the luxury of bread being now, however, omitted), for the benefit of certain hunters and trappers of an inferior standing; while the ordinary Canadian *engagés* were regaled on dried meat in one of their lodging rooms. . . .

We were sitting, on the following morning, in the passageway between the gates, conversing with the traders Vaskiss and May. These two men, together with our sleek friend, the clerk Monthalon, were, I believe, the only persons then in the fort who could read and write. May was telling a curious story about the traveler Catlin, when an ugly, diminutive Indian, wretchedly mounted, came up at a gallop, and rode by us into the fort. . . .

[He never finishes story about Catlin, which is interrupted by a visit of more Indians.]

These newcomers were scarcely arrived, when Bordeaux ran across the fort, shouting to his squaw to bring him his spyglass. The obedient Marie, the very model of a squaw, produced the instrument, and Bordeaux hurried with it to the wall. Pointing it eastward, he exclaimed, with an oath, that the families were coming. But a few moments elapsed before the heavy caravan of the emigrant wagons could be seen, steadily advancing from the hills. They gained the river, and, without turning or pausing, plunged in, passed through, and slowly ascending the opposing bank, kept directly on their way by the fort and the Indian village, until, gaining a spot a quarter of a mile distant, they wheeled into a circle. For some time our tranquillity was undisturbed. The emigrants were preparing their encampment; but no sooner was this accomplished, than Fort Laramie was taken by storm. A crowd of broad-brimmed hats, thin visages, and staring eyes, appeared suddenly at the gate. Tall, awkward men, in brown homespun; women, with cadaverous faces and long lank figures, came thronging in together, and, as if inspired by the very demon of curiosity, ransacked every nook and corner of the fort. Dismayed at this invasion, we withdrew in all speed to our chamber, vainly hoping that it might prove a sanctuary. The emigrants prosecuted their investigations with untiring vigor. They penetrated the rooms, or rather dens, inhabited by the astonished squaws. Resolved to search every mystery to the bottom, they explored the apartments of the men, and even that of Marie and the *bourgeois*. At last a numerous deputation appeared at our door, but found no encouragement to remain.

Having at length satisfied their curiosity, they next proceeded to business. The men occupied themselves in procuring supplies for their onward journey; either buying them, or giving in exchange superfluous articles of their own.

The emigrants felt a violent prejudice against the French Indians, as they called the trappers and traders. They thought, and with some reason, that these men bore them no goodwill. Many of them were firmly persuaded that the French were instigating the Indians to attack and cut them off. On visiting the encampment we were at once struck with the extraordinary perplexity and indecision that prevailed among them. They seemed like men totally out of their element; bewildered and amazed, like a troop of schoolboys lost in the woods. It was impossible to be long among them without being conscious of the bold spirit with which most of them were animated. But the *forest* is the home of the backwoodsman. On the remote prairie he is totally at a loss. He differs as much from the genuine "mountain man" as a Canadian voyageur, paddling his canoe on the rapids of the Ottawa, differs from an American sailor among the storms of Cape Horn. . . .

A full share of suspicion fell upon us. Being strangers, we were looked upon as enemies. Having occasion for a supply of lead and a few other necessary articles, we used to go over to the emigrant camps to obtain them. After some hesitation, some dubious glances, and fumbling of the hands in the pockets, the terms would be agreed upon, the price tendered, and the emigrant would go off to bring the article in question. After waiting until our patience gave out, we would go in search of him, and find him seated on the tongue of his wagon.

"Well, stranger," he would observe, as he saw us approach, "I reckon I won't trade."

Some friend of his had followed him from the scene of the bargain, and whispered in his ear that clearly we meant to cheat him, and he had better have nothing to do with us.

This timorous mood of the emigrants was doubly unfortunate, as it exposed them to real danger. Assume, in the presence of Indians, a bold bearing, self-confident yet vigilant, and you will find them tolerably safe neighbors. But your safety depends on the respect and fear you are able to inspire. If you betray timidity or indecision, you convert them from that moment into insidious and dangerous enemies. . . .

[In August the party reached Bent's Fort.]

Bent's Fort stands on the river, about seventy-five miles below the Pueblo. At noon of the third day we arrived within three or four miles of it, pitched our tent under a tree, hung our looking glasses against its trunk, and having made our primitive toilet, rode toward the fort. We soon came in sight of it, for it is visible from a considerable distance, standing with its high clay walls in the midst of the scorching plains. It seemed as if a swarm of locusts had invaded the country. The grass for miles around was cropped close by the horses of General Kearney's [sic] soldiery.

When we came to the fort, we found that not only had the horses eaten up the grass, but their owners had made way with the stores of the little trading post; so that we had great difficulty in procuring the few articles which we required for our homeward journey. The army was gone, the life and bustle passed away, and the fort was a scene of dull and lazy tranquillity.

A few invalid officers and soldiers sauntered about the area, which was oppressively hot; for the glaring sun was reflected down upon it from the high white walls around. The proprietors were absent, and we were received by Mr. Holt, who had been left in charge of the fort. He invited us to dinner, where, to our admiration, we found a table laid with a white cloth, with castors in the middle, and chairs placed around it. This unwonted repast concluded, we rode back to our camp.

Here, as we lay smoking round the fire after supper, we saw through the dusk three men approaching from the direction of the fort. They rode up and seated themselves near us on the ground. The foremost was a tall, well-formed man, with a face and manner such as inspire confidence at once. He wore a broad hat of felt, slouching and tattered, and the rest of his attire consisted of a frock and leggins of buckskin, rubbed with the yellow clay found among the mountains. At the heel of one of his moccasins was buckled a huge iron spur, with a rowel five or six inches in diameter. His horse, which stood quietly looking over his head, had a rude Mexican saddle, covered with a shaggy bearskin, and furnished with a pair of wooden stirrups of preposterous size. The next man was a sprightly, active little fellow, about five feet and a quarter high, but very strong and compact. His face was swarthy as a Mexican's, and covered with a close, curly, black beard. An old, greasy, calico handkerchief was tied around his head, and his close buckskin dress was blackened and polished by grease and hard service. The last who came up was a large, strong man, dressed in the coarse homespun of the frontiers, who dragged his long limbs over the ground as if he were too lazy for the effort. He had a sleepy gray eye, a retreating chin, an open mouth, and a protruding upper lip, which gave him an air of exquisite indolence and helplessness. He was armed with an old United States yager, which redoubtable weapon, though he could never hit his mark with it, he was accustomed to cherish as the very sovereign of firearms.

The first two men belonged to a party who had just come from California, with a large band of horses, which they had sold at Bent's Fort. Munroe, the taller of the two, was from Iowa. He was an excellent fellow, open, warm-hearted, and intelligent. Jim Gurney, the short man, was a Boston sailor, who had come in a trading vessel to California, and taken the fancy to return across the continent. The journey had already made him an expert "mountain man," and he presented the extraordinary phenomenon of a sailor who understood how to manage a horse. The third of our visitors, named Ellis, was a Missourian, who had come out with a party of Oregon emigrants, but having got as far as Bridger's Fort, he had fallen homesick, or as Jim averred, lovesick. He thought proper therefore to join the California men, and return homeward in their company.

They now requested that they might unite with our party, and make the journey to the settlements in company with us. We readily assented, for we liked the appearance of the first two men, and were very glad to gain so efficient a reinforcement. We told them to meet us on the next evening at a spot on the river side, about six miles below the fort. Having smoked a pipe together, our new allies left us, and we lay down to sleep. . . .

[By summer's end Parkman's adventure was over, and he and Shaw headed back to civilization.]

At length we saw the roof of a white man's dwelling between the opening trees. A few moments after, we were riding over the miserable log bridge that led into Westport. Westport had beheld strange scenes, but a rougher look-ing troop than ours, with our worn equipments and broken-down horses, was never seen even there. We passed the well-remembered tavern, Boone's grocery, and old Vogel's dram shop, and encamped on a meadow beyond. Here we were soon visited by a number of people who came to purchase our horses and equipments. This matter disposed of, we hired a wagon and drove to Kanzas landing. Here we were again received under the hospitable roof of our old friend Colonel Chick, and seated under his porch we looked down once more on the eddies of the Missouri.

Deslauriers made his appearance in the morning, strangely transformed by a hat, a coat, and a razor. His little log house was among the woods not far off. It seems he had meditated giving a ball in honor of his return, and had consulted Henry Chatillon, as to whether it would do to invite his *bourgeois*. Henry expressed his entire conviction that we would not take it amiss, and the invitation was now proffered accordingly, Deslauriers adding as a special inducement that Antoine Lajeunesse was to play the fiddle. We told him we would certainly come, but before evening the arrival of a steamboat from Fort Leavenworth prevented our being present at the expected festivities. Deslauriers was on the rock at the landingplace, waiting to take leave of us. . . .

We had taken leave of Munroe and Jim Gurney at Westport, and Henry Chatillon went down in the boat with us. The passage to St. Louis occupied eight days, during about a third of which time we were fast aground on sandbars. We passed the steamer *Amelia* crowded with a roaring crew of disbanded volunteers, swearing, drinking, gambling, and fighting. At length one evening we reached the crowded levee of St. Louis. Repairing to the Planters' House, we caused diligent search to be made for our trunks, which were at length discovered stowed away in the farthest corner of the storeroom. In the morning, transformed by the magic of the tailor's art, we hardly recognized each other.

On the evening before our departure, Henry Chatillon came to our rooms at the Planters' House to take leave of us. No one who met him in the streets of St. Louis would have taken him for a hunter fresh from the Rocky Mountains. He was very neatly and simply dressed in a suit of dark cloth; for although since his sixteenth year he had scarcely been for a month together among the abodes of men, he had a native good taste which always led him to pay great attention to his personal appearance. His tall athletic figure with its easy flexible motions appeared to advantage in his present dress; and his fine face, though roughened by a thousand storms, was not at all out of keeping with it. He had served us with a fidelity and zeal beyond all praise. We took leave of him with regret; and unless his changing features, as he shook us by the hand, belied him, the feeling on his part was no less than on ours. Shaw had given him a horse at Westport. My rifle, an excellent piece, which he had always been fond of using, is now in his hands, and perhaps at this moment its sharp voice is startling the echoes of the Rocky Mountains. On the next morning we left town, and after a fortnight of railroads, coaches, and steamboats, saw once more the familiar features of home.

[*The Oregon Trail* went through many editions. In the preface to the edition of 1892, Parkman mentions the changes that had taken place since 1846.]

In the preface to the fourth edition of this book, printed in 1872, I spoke of the changes that had already come over the Far West. Since that time change has grown to metamorphosis. For Indian teepees, with their trophies of bow, lance, shield, and dangling scalp locks, we have towns and cities, resorts of health and pleasure seekers, with an agreeable society, Paris fashions, the magazines, the latest poem, and the last new novel. The sons of civilization, drawn by the fascinations of a fresher and bolder life, thronged to the western wilds in multitudes which blighted the charm that had lured them.

The buffalo is gone, and of all his millions nothing is left but bones. Tame cattle and fences of barbed wire have supplanted his vast herds and boundless grazing grounds. Those discordant serenaders, the wolves that howled at evening about the traveler's campfire, have succumbed to

126

arsenic and hushed their savage music. The wild Indian is turned into an ugly caricature of his conqueror; and that which made him romantic, terrible, and hateful, is in large measure scourged out of him. The slow cavalcade of horsemen armed to the teeth has disappeared before parlor cars and the effeminate comforts of modern travel.

The rattlesnakes have grown bashful and retiring. The mountain lion shrinks from the face of man, and even grim "Old Ephraim," the grizzly bear, seeks the seclusion of his dens and caverns. It is said that he is no longer his former self, having found, by an intelligence not hitherto set to his credit, that his ferocious strength is no match for a repeating rifle; with which discovery he is reported to have grown diffident, and abated the truculence of his more prosperous days. One may be permitted to doubt if the bloodthirsty old savage has really experienced a change of heart; and before inviting him to single combat, the ambitious tenderfoot, though the proud possessor of a Winchester with sixteen cartridges in the magazine, would do well to consider not only the quality of his weapon, but also that of his own nerves.

He who feared neither bear, Indian, nor devil, the all-daring and all-enduring trapper, belongs to the past or lives only in a few gray-bearded survivals. In his stead we have the cowboy, and even his star begins to wane.

The Wild West is tamed, and its savage charms have withered. If this book can help to keep their memory alive, it will have done its part. It has found a powerful helper in the pencil of Mr. [Frederic] Remington, whose pictures are as full of truth as of spirit, for they are the work of one who knew the prairies and the mountains before irresistible commonplace had subdued them.

5

The Mountain Men*

ALTHOUGH the Lewis and Clark Expedition is the most famous of the explorations of the West, other official explorers of this early period also probed the distant interior of the continent in search of information about the land. For example, Lieutenant Zebulon Pike led two parties that covered vast distances. In the autumn of 1805 this youthful officer, then only twenty-six years old, left St. Louis with twenty men to attempt to find the headwaters of the Mississippi River. After wintering in Minnesota and making contacts with the Indians—and also with British fur traders who had beaten them to that region—they returned to St. Louis, where Pike was soon organizing another expedition to explore the Southwest. This time he led his men up the Missouri and across Kansas to the Republican River on the borders of southern Nebraska and across Colorado to the Rockies, where he went into winter quarters in 1806–7. He discovered but failed to climb Pikes Peak. From Colorado Pike moved on to the Rio Grande and New Mexico, where Mexican authorities arrested him and his men and carried them off to Chihuahua. At last the Mexicans marched them back to the borders of the United States in what is now the state of Louisiana. Pike had covered an enormous territory and accumulated considerable information, but for several years little came of it.

---

* A vivid account of the mountain men will be found in Robert G. Cleland, *This Reckless Breed of Men* (New York, 1950). This chapter owes much to that work.

Lieutenant Zebulon Pike. From a photograph of the portrait by C. W. Peale. Courtesy, Library of Congress.

An early view of the Rocky Mountains from the Platte River. From an engraving by F. Kearny after a drawing by S. Seymour, in E. James, *Account of an Expedition . . . to the Rocky Mountains . . . in 1819 & '20* (1822–23).

More significant than government-sponsored expeditions were the explorations of hundreds of trappers who probed rivers, creeks, lakes, and mountain passes throughout the West in the three decades following the return of Lewis and Clark. Indeed, as Lewis and Clark came down the Missouri on the last lap of their return journey, they met trappers and traders headed West. For many years to come, intrepid individuals wandered over endless expanses of the

Pike's Peak and Colorado City, about 1866. From a lithograph by J. Bien after a drawing by A. E. Mathews, in Mathews, *Pencil Sketches of Colorado* (1866).

West and passed on to others information useful to later immigrants and settlers. In some cases these individual trappers, who called themselves mountain men, led immigrants to the new territories. They also established contacts with the Indians and in some cases died at the hands of hostile warriors. Their stories constitute a dramatic portion of Western history.

The frontier town of St. Louis was the base from which organized fur companies, as well as independent traders, operated. The Missouri Fur Company, organized in 1809 by a Spanish-American named Manuel Lisa, had among its shareholders William Clark, Lewis' companion on the famous expedition to the Pacific, and two Frenchmen already experienced in Western trade, Auguste and Pierre Chouteau. This company, one of the first in the field, exploited the Rocky Mountain fur trade for several years and then retired to the lower Missouri when Indian hostility and the rivalry of British traders proved destructive. Other companies were soon active. The fur companies utilized the services of the mountain men, who were sometimes employees of the companies, sometimes independent trappers who sold their pelts where they chose.

One of the most famous fur-trading organizations was

Long Jacques, mountain man. From an engraving by W. G. Jackman in *New York Illustrated Magazine* (1846). Courtesy, New York Historical Society, New York City.

the American Fur Company, put together in 1808 by a German immigrant, John Jacob Astor, who laid the foundation of the vast Astor fortune. Astor conceived the notion of establishing a trading post at the mouth of the Columbia River, where his agents would collect beaver pelts from the Rocky Mountains and sea otter furs from the Pacific coast and ship them to China. The post that he established was Astoria. When British warships in the Pacific during the War of 1812 made the American position at Astoria untenable, Astor sold his Pacific trading post to a British outfit, the North West Company, and focused his attention on the relatively safe trade of the interior. Even here the Americans had to contend with rival British traders, notably the famous Hudson's Bay Company, whose agents already swarmed through the Northwest. At Fort Vancouver, in what is now southwestern Washington, this company had its Far Western headquarters, and there a giant of a man, famous in Western annals, Dr. John McLoughlin, ruled as superintendent.

Because the Hudson's Bay Company had established a firm base in the Northwest and the northern Rockies, American traders had to be content with the rivers and lakes of the central Rockies. In 1822 Major Andrew Henry

Fur traders on the Missouri attacked by hostile Indians. From a wood engraving after a sketch by W. M. Cary, in *Harper's Weekly* (May 23, 1868).

and William Henry Ashley organized a group to exploit the region now embraced by Montana, Wyoming, Idaho, Utah, and any adjacent territory that promised beaver skins. Eventually traders from this group developed the Rocky Mountain Fur Company.

For the next four years Henry and Ashley sent several hundred men, recruited from the riverfront of St. Louis and wherever they could find adventurous souls, into the Rocky Mountains in search of beaver skins. These partners also devised a new scheme for trading. Instead of having the trappers bring their catch all the way to St. Louis or to some trading post, Henry and Ashley had them come together at a rendezvous in the mountains where they sold their catch to the partners' agents and received goods and supplies for the next season. Ashley himself went into the mountains for the early rendezvous and in 1825 returned to St. Louis with a fortune in furs. Having got rich in this trade, Ashley made his last trip to the Rockies in 1826 and thereafter turned to politics. He managed to get himself elected to Congress and became an advocate in Washington of westward expansion.

Ashley, however, did not abandon an interest in the fur trade. Henceforth he would be a silent partner in the traffic, and to that end he sold an interest to three of his most enterprising leaders, Jedediah S. Smith, William L. Sublette, and David E. Jackson. Ashley agreed to stake them to supplies and equipment, and they agreed to sell exclusively to him. These three recruited parties of mountain men who were constantly searching for new territory where beaver abounded.

Of all the early mountain men, Jedediah Smith was one of the most daring. He performed incredible feats and his journeys took him through hitherto unknown terrain in the Far West. Born in Bainbridge, New York, and brought up with a smattering of classical learning, Smith found his way to St. Louis in time to join the first Henry-Ashley expedition to the Rockies in 1822. He quickly showed his mettle, learned the lore of the plains and mountains, proved a courageous Indian fighter, as well as a shrewd diplomat in dealing with the savages, and was given command of a group of trappers.

John Jacob Astor. From an engraving by Johnson, Fry & Co., after a painting by Alonzo Chappel (1864). Courtesy, Library of Congress.

Astor's trading post, Astoria, about the time it was sold to the British (1813). From a woodcut by Avery after a drawing by Parsons, in G. Franchere, *Narrative of a Voyage . . . 1814* (1854).

Astoria, renamed Fort George, in 1846. From a lithograph after a drawing by H. J. Warre, in Warre, *Sketches in North America* (1848).

Tough and hardened by mountain life, Smith managed to survive attacks by grizzly bears on more than one occasion. Once a grizzly laid open his scalp so that one ear hung by a shred of skin. His men were bewildered and uncertain about what to do, but weakened though he was by

134

loss of blood, Smith ordered one of the party, James Clyman, to get a needle and sew him up. When the impromptu surgeon came to the dangling ear, he could see no help for it. "You must try to stitch [it] up some way or other," Smith commanded. "I put in my needle," Clyman wrote in his diary, "stitching it through and through and over and over, laying the lacerated parts together as nice as I could with my hands." Miraculously, Smith recovered, and his ear grew back. Because of the hardiness of these mountain men, they sometimes survived injuries that would have killed lesser men. A celebrated mountain man named Peg Leg Smith got his name by amputating his own leg, which had been damaged by gunfire, and carving a peg leg from the limb of a tree.

Smith, Sublette, and Jackson agreed with Ashley to hold a rendezvous on Bear Lake, which extends across the borders of Idaho and Utah. This was in the heart of virgin beaver territory and offered a pleasant spot for meetings of the trappers. Other noted places for rendezvous were Jackson Hole (south of Yellowstone Park in Wyoming) and the Green River Valley in Utah.

After the winter and early spring trapping seasons were over, trappers, traders, and friendly Indians would meet at some well-watered spot where grass was plentiful for the horses, game was abundant, and the terrain was suitable for an encampment. Over distant trails, from far and near, trappers leading horses heavily burdened with packs of furs came to the rendezvous. Dressed in buckskin garments of their own creation, with hair and beards untrimmed, they made a wild and unruly appearance. Their deerskin jackets and trousers usually had fringes to decorate the edges. A hat or cap, made of coonskin or some other fur, topped their unkempt heads. Indian-style moccasins made of elkhide or buffalo skin served for shoes. The wilderness provided all the trappers needed in the way of garments, and the fit depended on their own skill with needle and awl. Sometimes a tailor could be found at the encamp-

Buildings of the American Fur Company at Fond du Lac, Wisconsin. From an engraving in T. A. McKenney, *Sketches of a Tour to the Lakes* (1827).

ments to make up a better-looking and better-fitting leather suit.

To the rendezvous came agents from St. Louis with knives, powder and shot, beaver traps, carbines, sugar, salt, coffee, tea, pepper, flour, blankets, bright cloth, and trinkets beloved by the Indian squaws whom the mountain men frequently took to wife, and, of course, tobacco, rum, and whiskey. For their goods, the agents thought nothing of charging nine times the price in St. Louis. Sugar, for example, usually sold for $1 per pound, coffee for $1.25, flour for $1.50, and rum for $13.50 per gallon. Some of the trappers were employees of the fur company and came to the rendezvous to turn over their furs and to receive their wages, which usually amounted to something on the order of $400 per year. Other trappers were independents, who sold their furs outright. Indians also brought furs, buffalo robes, and deerskins, which they bartered for the white man's wares.

After the distribution of a little rum and whiskey, excitement at the rendezvous picked up. The Indians' appetite for "firewater" was their undoing, for when they were a little drunk, unscrupulous traders diluted the drink with water and cheated them out of their furs for the least possible outlay in alcohol. The mountain men themselves frequently squandered their earnings on liquor, trinkets, and cloth for the Indian women or in gambling. Many a trapper for a few days in summer had a roaring orgy at the rendezvous and returned to the trapping country almost as poor as he had started. With luck he saved enough from his annual debauch to replenish his powder and shot, to buy a new skinning knife, and perhaps to obtain coffee and tobacco to last a few months.

After men had spent long months of solitary wandering in the wilderness, the rendezvous provided an opportunity for talk and the exchange of news. They swapped information about the best beaver streams and the meanest Indians, the spots where game was plentiful and the deserts where water and food could not be found. They marked in the dust trails they had followed, and they spun yarns about their adventures: the Indians they had tricked and foiled and the grizzlies they had shot.

Sports and pastimes took some of their time. They danced about their campfires much as the Indians did. They sang, sometimes bawdy tunes, but more often mournful hymns remembered from their dim past. Occasionally someone turned up with a fiddle or a mouth organ to pro-

Mountain men setting traps for beavers. From a watercolor by A. J. Miller. *Courtesy, Walters Art Gallery.*

Rendezvous at Green River, 1837, attended by Jim Bridger, Kit Carson, and others. From a painting by A. J. Miller. *Courtesy, Walters Art Gallery.*

vide music. There were trials of skill or strength, wrestling, jumping, and footraces. Always there were demonstrations of marksmanship, sometimes while riding at a wild gallop. If the Indians were friendly, the trappers visited their lodges, gravely smoked with the elders, and made friends with the prettiest girls. The lonely winter was a long way off, and now all was gaiety and merriment.

But not always did the rendezvous end on an idyllic note. Liquor made bad actors out of both trappers and Indians, and fights frequently occurred. Sometimes a whole group of mountain men full of liquor fell to battering one another with their fists, gouging eyes, and stomping the men who were down, for anything was fair in a fight of this sort. Occasionally fights ended in gunfire, and one or more corpses lay stretched on the grass when the combatants sobered up and looked about them.

After a few days or weeks, as the case might be, the rendezvous ended and wagons or packtrains laden with pelts headed East. The trappers loaded their property, which they called their possibles, onto the backs of horses if they had such animals or on their own backs if they had gambled away their pack animals and once more vanished into the distant plains, mountains, and woods.

The rendezvous was not the only center where traders from the East collected furs. Gradually regular trading posts, essentially fortified places in the Indian country, came into being. One of the first and the most important of

Trappers with their "possibles" set out again for the beaver hunt. From a Miller painting. Courtesy, Walters Art Gallery.

Fort Union and distribution of goods to the Assiniboins. From a lithograph by Sarony, Major & Knapp after a drawing by Stanley. Courtesy, Library of Congress.

the early trading posts was Fort Lisa, named for Manuel Lisa of St. Louis, who founded it in 1812 near the present site of Omaha, Nebraska. Other important trading posts were Fort Union, established by the American Fur Company in 1829 on the Missouri River not far from its confluence with the Yellowstone; Fort Pierre, near the present city of Pierre, South Dakota; and Bent's Fort, some 80 miles northeast of Taos, New Mexico, near La Junta, Colorado. Many other trading posts and forts were established by fur traders in the Indian country, but these were typical.

The fortified stockade of Fort Laramie, in the Sioux country (now Wyoming), 1837.

Long before the government of the United States got around to stationing garrisons in the West to protect the frontier, the fortified trading posts of the fur traders served that purpose. Some of the traders had great influence with the Indians and managed by diplomacy, mixed with an occasional display of armed might, to maintain a semblance of peace. The Spanish-American Manuel Lisa, for example, though accused of encouraging Indians to attack rival traders, was called upon by Governor William Clark during the War of 1812 to keep British-inspired Indians from going on the warpath—a feat that he accomplished.

The frontier trading posts were strongly fortified stockades, designed to resist sudden Indian attacks or even a long siege. In a characteristic type of construction, the walls, made of upended logs, pierced at intervals with loopholes for cannon or rifle fire, had the further protection of blockhouses at the corners. From these blockhouses light cannon, loaded with grapeshot, could sweep the fields beyond the walls or, in case of a sudden uprising within the fort, the courtyards below. A heavy postern gate, wide enough to admit wagons, was the one entrance to the fort. A small door in one side of the great gate admitted one person or one horse at a time. This door was the only one usually open. A strongly built warehouse inside the stockade held surplus trading goods and packs of furs awaiting shipment back to St. Louis. A large trading house with a great fireplace at one end and benches along the walls contained samples of the trading goods available and sometimes had a bar where drinks were dispensed. Here trappers and traders mingled, swapped yarns, and made their deals. Here, too, Indians were admitted, as many as the commander of the post thought discreet. Here on occasion were held dances and frolics in which Indian women joined.

Other buildings in the stockade contained living quarters, the kitchen, and the dining hall for officers and men of the post. Here came invited guests to live for a time on the hospitality of the traders. Outside the stockade Indians pitched their tepees. Trappers were content to spread

Fort Laramie interior. Both from paintings by Miller. *Courtesy, Walters Art Gallery.*

A garrison of government troops defending a stockade against Indians. From a photograph of a painting by Schreyvogel. *Courtesy, Library of Congress.*

their blankets on any convenient floor. Houses inside the stockade usually had roofs covered with turf to protect them against fire in case of an Indian attack. Flaming arrows would fall harmlessly on the surface of earth.

Bent's Fort was one of the best-known and best-defended strongholds of the traders in the West. Built by Charles and William Bent and a picturesque Frenchman, Céran St. Vrain, it became a center for trade with the whole Southwest. Santa Fe was near enough for both legal and illegal traffic with that Mexican metropolis, and the unexploited rivers of Utah, Idaho, and Wyoming poured a rich stream of beaver pelts into Bent's Fort. William Bent took to wife Owl Woman, daughter of White Thunder, an important chief of the Cheyenne tribe. This marriage helped keep peace with the powerful Cheyennes and other Plains Indians. The Bents and St. Vrain could send their wagon trains to St. Louis with little fear that they would be pillaged on the way.

Unlike some of the other trading posts, Bent's Fort was

built of adobe (sun-dried brick) with walls 15 feet high and 7 feet thick at the base. Two round towers 30 feet high stood out from the walls at the northwest and southeast corners. Cannon mounted in the towers could sweep every point of attack, and no enemy could creep up beneath the walls. In another watchtower over the entrance a guard constantly swept the plains with a long telescope. The traders ran no risk of a surprise attack.

Mexicans from Taos and Santa Fe brought flour, corn, beans, squash, dried pumpkins, salt, and pepper, which they bartered for tobacco, cloth, coffee, sugar, guns, and ammunition. The resident traders collected buffalo robes, deerhides, and an occasional bearskin from the Indians; from the free trappers, they accumulated beaver pelts, which they pressed into bales for shipment East.

The Bents and St. Vrain began building their fort in 1828 and completed it in 1832. Until 1852 it was the most important outpost in the Southwest and did much to assure

Bents Fort, about 1846. From a lithograph by E. Weber & Co. Courtesy, *Library of Congress.*

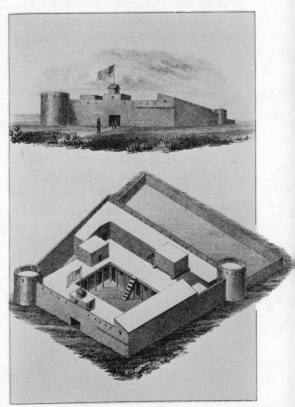

the success of the United States' penetration of the region. The Bents and St. Vrain maintained good relations with the Mexican authorities at Santa Fe until the approach of the Mexican War, though from time to time the Mexicans complained about smugglers being harbored at the fort and about trade in contraband goods. In 1852, after the California gold rush made frontier forts of greater importance for the protection of immigrants, the United States government tried to buy Bent's Fort, but the offered price was so low that William Bent chose instead to blow it up with gunpowder. He then built another fortified trading post farther down the Arkansas River.

Although the fortified trading posts were significant in the development of the West, many of the hardened mountain men preferred the free life at the annual rendezvous, and this system lasted as long as the beaver trade remained profitable. From the annual rendezvous went out many of the trappers who discovered the routes later followed by immigrant trains. Of the trappers who followed the beaver wherever their signs might lead, few were more enterprising than Jedediah Smith who made two extraordinary journeys to the Pacific coast.

Smith's first journey began on August 26, 1826, when he and seventeen other trappers set out from the Bear River on the Utah-Idaho border to discover new beaver streams in the West. Without maps or accurate information about the land ahead of them, they made their way southwest through Utah and Arizona, over deserts and mountains to the Colorado River. After following it for a short distance, they struck across the desert to the Mojave River, which Smith named the "Inconstant" because at intervals the water disappeared under the desert sand. Reaching a sort of oasis where the Mojave Indians grew corn, melons, and vegetables, Smith and his men traded for fresh food and rested until they could gather strength for the remainder of their journey across the California desert. After a hard climb over the San Bernardino Mountains, the trappers

144

Typical architecture of a California mission. From a photograph (n.d.) in the collections of the Library of Congress.

The village of Los Angeles, 1853–54. From *Reports of Explorations and Surveys, 1853-'54* (1856).

at last emerged into a fertile plain where thousands of cattle and horses grazed. On November 27, three months and a day after leaving their camp in the Bear Valley, they reached the Franciscan mission of San Gabriel, southeast of the tiny village of Los Angeles. They were the first citizens of the United States to cross the American continent to reach California, though American ships were already engaged in the hide and tallow trade.

The mission fathers received the ragged and dirty wanderers hospitably, but they were less than welcome to the

145

governor of the territory, who ordered them to return whence they had come. Since they had no passports and no licenses to trap in Spanish territory, they were subject to arrest, but the governor thought the easiest way out would be to let the interlopers go of their own accord.

The trappers took their time and rested comfortably at the mission, a patriarchal establishment where the Franciscans had gathered the Indians and were attempting to show them the way to heaven by first indoctrinating them in the ways of the white man's civilization. To Smith's men, who had long lived on nothing except the meat of wild game, and sometimes little of that, the bountiful bread, beef, fruit, and wine of the mission were luxuries beyond belief. Christmas found them still enjoying the mission's hospitality, sometimes to the fathers' embarrassment. On Twelfth Night, for example, James Reed, the blacksmith in the party, drank too much wine and brandy and created a disturbance at dinner, but "the padre, seeing he was in a state of inebriety," reported one of the trappers, "refrained from saying anything."

At last the trappers moved on to a mission outpost near the present town of Redlands, California, and spent a week preparing for their return journey. They were now out of reach of the governor and had no notion of retracing their outward route. The interior of California, unpopulated and unexplored by Americans, was too tempting. After gathering horses and obtaining a quantity of dried beef, on February 1, 1827, they crossed the San Bernardino Mountains again and marched north until they found a pass in the Tehachapi Mountains that led them eventually into the San Joaquin Valley, which teemed with deer, elk, bear, wild ducks, and geese, and, of course, the prized beaver. Hunting and trapping, they made their way up the San Joaquin River and then followed a tributary, the Stanislaus, to the foothills of the Sierras. They could see the high peaks of the snow-covered mountains, over

which they had to find a pass. Leaving the main party encamped on the western side of the mountains, Smith and
two companions made their way over the mountains in
late May and crossed the desolate and waterless stretch
of the Great Salt Lake Desert on foot. The last of their
horses had already died, and they had eaten its stringy
flesh. Finally, more dead than alive, on July 3, the three
stumbled into the Bear Valley and joined colleagues whom
they had left nearly a year before.

Waiting only ten days to recuperate, Smith organized
another party of eighteen men and, on July 13, 1827, again
set out for the West, to rejoin his men on the Stanislaus and
to explore further the country northward and westward to
the Pacific. He followed much the same route into California that he had taken the previous year, but this time
the Mojave Indians proved hostile and treacherous. While
Smith's men were swimming their horses and ferrying
their goods over the Colorado, the Indians attacked, killing ten men outright and leaving another desperately
wounded. Fleeing to a clump of trees, the survivors prepared to sell their lives as dearly as possible. When the Indians attacked, Smith's marksmen picked off three with
their first volley, and the rest of the Indians fled.

With scanty supplies and little ammunition, Smith and
his remaining companions struggled across the desert for
nine days until they reached the foothills of the mountains
and found friendly Indians who sold them horses for a few
trinkets. They then crossed the mountains over the Cajon
Pass into a land of green pasturage, where they killed a
few fat beeves to replenish their food supply. This time,
lest they incur the wrath of the California governor a second time, they avoided San Gabriel and headed northward
for the San Joaquin Valley. On September 18, 1827, Smith
and five men reached the original party on the Stanislaus.
Ten men had died under the arrows of the Mojave Indians; the wounded man, whom the trappers had car-

ried across the desert, was left to find his way to San Gabriel, and two others had also remained behind in the San Gabriel Valley.

If Smith thought he could avoid trouble with the governor of California, he was mistaken. Short of supplies, he appealed to the mission at San Jose for help, but the father there regarded him and his men as spies and turned them over to the civil authorities at Monterey. Yankee ship captains, however, came to their rescue, bought 1,600 pounds of beaver pelts at $2.50 a pound (perhaps half of what they would have been worth at the rendezvous), and gave bond for the trappers' departure from California. Encouraged by the bond, the governor even supplied ammunition, clothing, and trade goods.

Smith and his men did not attempt to leave California by crossing eastward, as the authorities expected them to do; instead, they continued northward through the Sacramento Valley, hoping eventually to find a gap in the Sierras. Beaver and game were plentiful, and they continued to accumulate pelts despite a scarcity of traps and the torrential rains that flooded the valley and threatened to drown them in a vast quagmire.

Plodding slowly northward, the party reached the border of Oregon in late May, crossed the Rogue River, and reached the Pacific coast at Coos Bay. By July 13 they had traveled up the Umpqua River and pitched camp on a tributary, where they allowed the Umpqua Indians to flock to the camp for trade. Smith and two other men were away at the time, examining the country beyond. Taking advantage of the trappers' carelessness, the Indians suddenly fell upon them and slaughtered all except one man who escaped to the woods and ultimately made his way to the Hudson's Bay post at Fort Vancouver. Smith and his two companions also sought refuge at Vancouver.

The superintendent of Fort Vancouver, Dr. John McLoughlin, sent an expedition in pursuit of the Umpqua Indians and reclaimed some of the stolen furs, which Smith

Fort Vancouver, Washington Territory, about 1848. From a lithograph in Warre's *Sketches*.

sold to the Hudson's Bay Company for $3,200. Smith and the other three survivors spent the ensuing winter at Vancouver. In gratitude they provided Dr. McLoughlin with information about the streams they had explored, and one of the men served as guide for trapping parties. Dr. McLoughlin's kindness paid dividends, for Smith did his best to encourage a friendly feeling for the great company on the part of rival American trappers.

With the coming of spring, Smith and one companion, a huge man named Black, the one survivor of the Umpqua massacre, set out on the lonely and dangerous journey from Vancouver across seemingly endless ranges of mountains to the appointed place of rendezvous in Jackson Hole. None who saw them depart expected they would ever reach their destination. But by some miracle both men escaped death from cold, grizzlies, Indians, thirst, starvation, and other perils of wilderness and desert and managed to reach northwestern Montana. There they met a party of trappers searching for them, and thus reinforced, they went on to a new place of rendezvous at Pierre's Hole, west of the Grand Tetons. The journey that had begun in July, 1827, had ended in the summer of 1829. Smith had traversed an immense area through the modern states of Utah, Nevada, California, Oregon, Washington, Montana, Idaho, and Wyoming. Because of the Umpqua massacre, the expedition had been a disaster, but Smith brought back a stock of valuable information, which he made available to his colleagues in the fur trade. He and Black even arrived at the rendezvous with enough furs taken on the way to make them solvent.

The first wagon train over the Oregon Trail, 1830. A reconstruction of Smith, Jackson, and Sublette en route to the rendezvous at Wind River, with ten wagons, five mules each, and eighty-two men. From a photograph of a painting by W. H. Jackson (1930). *Courtesy, Library of Congress.*

In July, 1830, Smith and his partners, Jackson and Sublette, held their last rendezvous, this time on the Wind River in Wyoming, and returned to St. Louis with furs and mules which a newspaper at the time reported to be worth $15,000. The partners sold their interest in the fur trade to the Rocky Mountain Fur Company and proposed to retire from active life in the mountains.

After the freedom of the wilds, Smith found civilization oppressive, and in the spring of 1831 he once more took the trail, this time with a wagon train bound for Santa Fe. When the train lost its way in the desert, Smith rode ahead to try to find water and at last reached the Cimarron River, which, like the Mojave, had disappeared under the sand. While Smith was digging a hole in the riverbed in search of water, a marauding band of Comanche Indians attacked, and Smith died at their hands. Thus ended the life of one of the most famous and courageous of the pathfinders of the West.

Although few men equaled the exploits of Jedediah Smith, other mountain men left their mark on the history of the West. Some were useful pathfinders like Smith; others were colorful and exotic characters who became part of the folklore of the country. Next to Smith, Joseph R. Walker contributed more than any other to the early knowledge of the Southwest. Posterity has given his name to Walker Pass in California, the Walker River in California and Nevada, and Walker Lake in Nevada. For two decades and more this gaunt Tennesseean explored the whole Southwest. In 1832 Captain Benjamin Louis Eulalie de Bonneville, a French-born officer in the United States Army, whose exploits in the West attracted the interest of Washington Irving, engaged Walker as one of his captains and guides. From this time on Walker was constantly engaged in expeditions of trade and exploration. The story of his adventures reads much like the hardships and adventures of Smith and his men.

Other mountain men who have left their names on the landscape include one of the strangest eccentrics, Old Bill Williams, a renegade preacher from the Missouri frontier, who by preference trapped alone and wandered through the wildest part of Arizona and New Mexico in search of beaver with no companion except his horse. Occasionally, however, he was persuaded to join some exploring or trapping party. Since he had married an Osage woman and had been adopted into the tribe, he proved useful in 1825 to a United States commission surveying a route to Santa Fe, for he could serve as both a guide and a go-between with the Osages. He joined Joseph Walker's expedition to California in 1833–34 and was employed by John Charles Frémont to guide his ill-fated expedition of 1848–49 over the mountains of New Mexico. Unfortunately Frémont ignored Old Bill's advice and lost eleven men in the snow. When trying to salvage some of Frémont's instruments and goods during the following spring, Williams was killed by Indians. By this time he had already become a legend for his reputed strength, his ability to go off alone and come back safely with a valuable pack of furs, and his prodigious orgies at a mountain rendezvous. He gave his name to an Arizona town, a tributary of the Colorado River, and a mountain peak.

By about 1840 the best period of beaver trapping was over. A change of fashion in Europe had ruined the trade. For the previous four decades, tall hats made of beaver fur had been the required wear for any man who wanted to be in style. But by 1840 silk from China had begun to replace beaver felt as the preferred material for fashionable hats. Silk was lighter and, in the eyes of most men now, better-looking. So silk hats saved the lives of thousands of beaver and forced many mountain men to other occupations. Furthermore, immigrants were driving their ox wagons across the plains in search of new homes in the West. The trails that the mountain men had blazed would now be followed by homesteaders in search of better land and a prosperity that Americans found ever beckoning in the West.

Life in Primitive Los Angeles
(1850)

A young Army lieutenant, E. Gould Buffum, in 1850 wrote a firsthand account of life in California, published in that year under the title *Six Months in the Gold Fields . . . from a Journal of Three Years Residence in Upper and Lower California, 1847–8–9*. Although most of the book consists of an account of adventures in the gold-mining region, he gave a description of Los Angeles when it was a sleepy settlement where some of the pioneering mountain men had occasionally found refreshment.

One hundred and ten miles south of Santa Barbara is the Pueblo de los Angelos (City of the Angels), the garden spot of California. It is situated at the end of an immense plain, which extends from San Pedro, the port of the Pueblo twenty-five miles distant, to this point. As in all California towns, the houses are built of adobe and are covered with an asphaltum, which is found in great quantities issuing from the ground near the town. The northern portion of the town is laid out in streets, and appropriated as the residence of the trading citizens, while the southern part is made up of gardens, vineyards, and orchards. Through all these a large stream runs, which is used to irrigate the soil. The vineyards are lovely spots; acres upon acres of ground are covered with vines, which are trimmed every year, and thus kept about six feet in height, and in the fall of the year are hanging thick with clusters of grapes. In addition to these, apples, pears, peaches, plums, and figs are raised in great abundance. An American, named Wolfskill, has here a vineyard containing thirty thousand bearing grapevines, from which he makes annually a thousand barrels of wine and two or three hundred of *aguardiente*, the brandy of the country. Some of this wine is a very superior article, resembling in its flavor the best Madeira, while another kind, the *vino tinto*, is execrable stuff. With proper care and apparatus, however, the grape of the Pueblo could be made to yield as good wine as any in the world; and the whole plain, twenty-five miles in extent, reaching to the beach at San Pedro, is susceptible of the cultivation of the vine.

Until the late astonishing growth of San Francisco, the Pueblo was the largest town in California, containing about two thousand inhabitants, who are principally wealthy rancheros and those who reside there to cultivate the grape. Game of many kinds abounds in the vicinity of the Pueblo. During the rainy season, the plains in the direction of San Pedro are covered with millions of geese and ducks, which are shot by the dozen, while the surrounding hills afford an abundance of quails, deer, elk, and antelope.

The inhabitants of the Pueblo are of the better and wealthier class of Californians, and have always been strongly disposed towards the institutions of Mexico; and at the time of the conquest of California, they fought with a determined resistance against the naval forces of Commodore Stockton. They have now, however, become reconciled to the institutions of our country, and will, I doubt not, in a few years make as good a set of democrats as can be found in Missouri or Arkansas. They are very strongly attached to the Roman Catholic Church, and are probably the most "religious," in their acceptation of the term, of any people in California. Every morning the solemn toll of the church bell calls them to mass; at noon it is rung again, and every Poblano at the sound doffs his sombrero and remains reverently uncovered in the hot sun, while the bell reminds him that he is to mutter over a short prayer. In whatever avocation they may be engaged, whether fiddling, dancing, singing, slaughtering cattle, or playing billiards or monte, the custom is invariably followed. I have seen a party in a tavern in the Pueblo, busily engaged in betting against a monte bank, when the noonday bell tolled; a fellow, with his last dollar in the world placed upon a card, immediately doffed his hat and muttered his prayer; the dealer laid down his cards and did the same, and they continued in their humble positions till the bell ceased tolling, when the game and the swearing went on as busily as usual.

About ten miles from Los Angelos is the mission of San Gabriel, located upon the river of that name, whose banks for miles are girdled with grapevines. This is one of the prettiest spots in California and affords a fine opportunity for the raising of fruit. The country around the Pueblo is by far the most favorable portion of southern California for the settlement of foreigners. Possessing a climate of unequaled mildness and a soil of great fertility, it must inevitably, ere long, be surrounded by a large population.

6

Gold Fever*

TALES that mountain men brought back about California and the Northwest stirred restless folk in Missouri, Illinois, Iowa, and settlements all along the Midwestern frontier zone to contemplate emigration over the mountains. The great quantities of cowhides and tallow available in California had already attracted New England shipmasters to that coast, and Richard Henry Dana's *Two Years Before the Mast* and other contemporary writings described the land as one of eternal springtime. Shipmasters bound for China had long been familiar with the Oregon coast, where they picked up cargoes of sea otter furs.

By the 1830's Americans were talking of moving to Oregon, and in 1834 a small body of missionaries, intent upon saving the souls of the Indians, settled in the Willamette Valley. Two years later the missionary group was reinforced by another party led to Oregon by a physician, Dr. Marcus Whitman. The Oregon Trail from Independence, Missouri, up the Platte River by Fort Laramie, South Pass, Fort Hall on the Snake River, Fort Boise to Walla Walla

* An excellent account of gold mining in California in all its aspects will be found in Rodman W. Paul, *California Gold* (Cambridge, Mass., 1947).

The Oregon Trail, 1846. From a map compiled for the U.S. Department of Public Roads (1938). *Courtesy, Map Division of the Library of Congress.*

and down the Columbia River, which these missionaries followed, was soon to become one of the great highways for Western homesteaders.

By the 1840's small groups of immigrants were trickling over desert and mountain trails into California, a Mexican province, that somewhat grudgingly allowed them to settle. In 1846 the ill-fated Donner party was caught in an early blizzard in the Sierras, and seventy-nine men, women, and children were marooned in the snowpacked mountains. Thirty-four died from exposure or starvation. But not even news of that catastrophe discouraged frontier families eager to reach a land described as a paradise.

The Mexican War in 1846–48 changed the sovereignty of the Western country and placed the Mexican provinces under the jurisdiction of the United States. The way was now open for increased immigration into California and other Western territories. Suddenly in 1848 occurred an event that electrified the whole of the United States and started a vast avalanche of immigrants to the West Coast. Gold was discovered in California.

Some gold had been dug out of the hills of southern California by the Spaniards; but no startling strikes had been made, and little attention was paid to the possibility of mineral wealth in that sleepy province of Mexico. The Spanish settlers had been content to lead a good life as proprietors of baronial ranches, where they raised cattle, horses, and mules by the thousands and lived in ease and comfort. A few Americans had married into Spanish families and had also become great landowners, but they, too, saw no possibilities in mining.

The discovery of gold that precipitated the great California gold rush was made by a workman named James W. Marshall on January 24, 1848, in the tailrace of a sawmill on the American River at Coloma, about 40 miles from the modern city of Sacramento. The land was owned by a German Swiss, Johann August Sutter, who had obtained from the Mexican authorities a large grant in the wilderness. He erected a fort near the site of Sacramento, and this base became one of the most powerful strongholds on the frontier.

When Marshall picked up the nuggets of gold in Sutter's

Independence, Missouri, in the mid-nineteenth century. From an engraving after H. J. Meyer, in C. A. Dana, *United States Illustrated* (c. 1855). Courtesy, Library of Congress.

Sweetwater River and Devil's Gate on the Oregon Trail, approximately as it was in 1830. From a photograph of a painting by Jackson (1930). *Courtesy, Library of Congress.*

millrace, he little knew that his action would have worldwide repercussions. He told Sutter what he had found, and they agreed to say nothing about the discovery. Sutter was afraid his workmen might go off in search of gold instead of sticking to their labors in his wheat fields, sawmill, and cattle ranch. But such news could not be kept secret.

Rumors began to circulate that somebody had made a gold strike on Sutter's land. Near the end of May the news broke in Monterey that gold had been found on the American River. Immediately everybody was talking about the gold strike, and soon excitement reached a fever pitch. Prospectors went out to search for themselves and came back with veritable proof in the form of heavy gold nuggets. By the end of June, everybody in Monterey and the surrounding country had heard the glad tidings and was trying to get to the goldfields.

An entry of June 20, 1848, in the diary kept by Walter Colton, the mayor of Monterey, gives this graphic picture: "The excitement produced was intense and many were soon busy in their hasty preparations for a departure to the mines. The family who had kept house for me caught the moving infection. Husband and wife were both packing up. The blacksmith dropped his hammer, the carpenter his plane, the mason his trowel, the farmer his sickle, the baker his loaf, and the tapster his bottle. All were off for the mines, some on horses, some on carts, and some on crutches, and one went in a litter. An American woman who had recently established a boarding house here pulled up stakes and went off before her lodgers had even time to pay their bills. . . . I have only a community of women left, and a gang of prisoners with here and there a soldier who will give his captain the slip at the first chance." This quotation is cited by Robert G. Cleland in *A History of*

Independence Rock on the Oregon Trail. The famous landmark between Fort Laramie and South Pass served as an autograph rock where hundreds of emigrants inscribed their names, some of which are visible today. From a contemporary painting by Miller (c. 1837). *Courtesy, Walters Art Gallery.*

Sutter's Fort, Sacramento, California, in 1847. From a lithograph by S. Shannan in the collection of the Library of Congress.

California: The American Period (1922), which gives a valuable and succinct account of the gold rush.

With a few months word had spread throughout California, and a stampede for the gold country began. Men deserted farms and ranches, shops, offices, and businesses and streamed north to the American River. Ships that put into San Francisco Bay lost their crews and even their officers. Some vessels were left swinging at anchor with no living thing on board except the captain's cat. Soldiers deserted from the tiny garrisons, and such law officers as the settlements boasted joined the throng. Women and children also went along; everybody who could get a pick, shovel, and a pan in which to wash the dirt-bearing gold headed for the goldfields, dreaming of sudden wealth.

For a time, dreams did come true. River sand and pockets of earth in the hillside yielded gold. Men picked up lumps of gold like pebbles in potholes in the streams. There in time past the heavy gold had sunk to the bottom, as the sand and light earth had washed away. Some of the gold appeared as tiny, heavy flakes that sank to the bottom of a pan when gold-bearing earth was washed. This type, collected as gold dust, was stored in small buckskin bags or sometimes in hollow quills made from the wing feathers of vultures and eagles. Lumps, or nuggets, from the size of a

A gold-mining scene in California. From a Currier & Ives lithograph (1871). *Courtesy, Library of Congress.*

pea to a few as big as an egg or even larger, came to light as miners feverishly dug into the hills, washed the dirt away, and looked for the shining metal.

The richness of the loose gold, either dust or nuggets, during the early days of discovery was enough to excite anyone. "Two men in seven days obtained $17,000 from a trench a few feet wide and a hundred feet long," Cleland wrote. "Ten men made $1,500 each in ten days. A single miner obtained two pounds and a half of gold in fifteen minutes. A group of Mexicans were seen gambling with a hundred pounds of gold dust and nuggets serving as the 'bank.' In less than half an hour a man picked between five and six ounces of gold 'out of an open hole in the rock, as fast as one can pick the kernels out of a lot of cracked shell barks.' . . . The striking thing about the mining industry as it was carried out for the first few months, however, was not the lucky finds of a few but the assured profit for practically everyone who engaged in it. The average return was from $10 to $50 a day, and by August it was reliably estimated that $600,000 had been secured from the various 'diggings.' " Since money was worth much more in these preinflation days than now, and the normal wage for a laborer was $1 a day, a return of from $10 to $50 for a day's digging looked like the way to wealth.

Although no telegraph or telephone, radio or television existed in this early time, the news of the gold strike in California soon spread like a prairie fire to distant parts of the world. By the end of 1849 would-be gold miners, from all over the United States, South America, Europe, Australia, the Hawaiian Islands, China, and heaven only knows where else, were swarming to California. Beginning in the summer of 1848, newspapers in the United States had begun to print exaggerated reports of the wealth to be found in the goldfields, and before the end of the year men from all parts of the country were streaming West in wagon trains, on horses and mules, or even on foot. Although the majority were men without women, some set out with their families.

Ships sailing around Cape Horn for the West Coast were overloaded with passengers willing to pay any price or risk any danger to get there. Other ships bound for Central America had more passengers than they could easily accommodate, for these travelers hoped to cross the Isthmus of Panama or Nicaragua to a western port in the expectation of picking up a ship for California. Others landed at Veracruz and made their way across Mexico to Acapulco on the Pacific side of Mexico, whence they tried to find a vessel bound north. A few were so desperate that they tried to sail or row from the coast of Mexico in open boats. The gold fever left men crazed and desperate.

The route across Central America offered deadly perils. Not only was the country a dismal swamp, populated by Indians and devoid of adequate accommodations for travelers, but its steaming jungles also harbored swarms of mosquitoes and snakes. Malaria, yellow fever, dysentery, and

162

cholera all took their toll of California-bound immigrants who chose this route. Strange to say, many got through and eventually reached the promised land.

But by far the largest number of gold seekers went overland from frontier staging areas in Missouri: St. Louis, Independence, or some other outfitting point. Whole families departed, for they were going to stay in the El Dorado of the West. Long lines of ox wagons of the type known as prairie schooners, hundreds of packhorses, and droves of cattle stretched out across the plains, ever creeping westward from the summer of 1848 for several years to come. These families took along such possessions as they would need in the new country: utensils, tools, household furniture, even heavy bureaus and bedsteads, foodstuffs, and clothing. A few carried books for instruction or entertainment. Not many of the immigrants realized the hardships and dangers ahead of them, but no hazard could deter victims of gold fever.

They followed the trails that the mountain men had discovered, and immigrant parties frequently managed to find some scout or trapper to guide them across deserts and mountains. Other groups, less fortunate or less cautious, struck out alone and occasionally attempted short cuts to the goldfields. One such party in the autumn of 1849, trying to find a direct route across the mountains, landed in a desolate waste of sand and salt flats east of Owens Lake. Short of water and food, they brought up against the sheer walls of Death Valley and could not find their way out. Two of the strongest young men in the party, William Lewis Manly and John Rogers, volunteered to go on foot in search of a pass over the mountains and a settlement beyond, where they hoped to find aid. They left a small party of more than a dozen adults and several small children who huddled disconsolate in the shade of their wagons with little hope of getting out alive. No grass for their oxen could be found, and only a little brackish water kept them from dying of thirst. Many years later Manly wrote down an account of his and Rogers' journey and the ultimate rescue of the marooned immigrants. This narrative, *Death Valley in '49* (1894), is an epic of misery—and of courage.

Manly and Rogers themselves nearly perished trying to reach the Mexican settlements west of the mountains. "We were so nearly worn out that we tried to eat a little meat [dried beef], but after chewing a long time, the mouth would not moisten it enough so we could swallow and we had to reject it," Manly wrote in describing one portion of their march across the waterless waste. "The thought of the women and children waiting for our return made us feel more desperate than if we were the only ones concerned. We thought we could fight to the death over a water hole if we could only secure a little of the precious fluid. No one who has never felt the extreme of thirst can imagine the distress, the despair, which it brings."

The two men struggled on, sometimes more dead than alive. Along the way they noticed two or three dead bodies of men who had earlier left the party to try to find their way out alone. But eventually the two reached the San Fernando Mission, obtained a little food, a blind mule and two

An emigrant family like Sarah Royce's, crossing the plains. From an engraving by H. B. Hall, Jr., after a drawing by F. O. C. Darley (1869). *Courtesy, Library of Congress.*

Wagon trains were attacked by Indians day and night. From a photograph of a painting by Frederic Remington. *Courtesy, Library of Congress.*

horses, and started the return journey to lead their companions out of Death Valley. The story of how they reached the party as they had abandoned hope, how they led men, women, and children back over a weary expanse of alkali flats, narrow defiles in the hills, miles of sharp stones that cut their moccasins to pieces, waterless camps, and of their ultimate rescue by friendly Mexicans in the San Fernando Valley is a revelation of what human beings can endure.

Other wagon trains also were lost and suffered tragedy. Sometimes Indians drove off oxen and horses, leaving the hapless immigrants stranded. Sometimes the savages slaughtered the travelers in a sudden attack and made off with their possessions. The westward overland journey was one of terrible hardship and suffering. Yet thousands undertook the adventure.

Many accounts of the westward crossing have survived in diaries and journals of the travelers. One of the most fascinating is a diary kept by Sarah Royce, mother of Josiah Royce, who became one of the great teachers of philosophy at Harvard. Mrs. Royce, her husband, and her two-year-old daughter left eastern Iowa in the spring of 1849 and finally reached Grass Valley, California, late in October. Her account of their trials and near death on the way is another vivid description of the fortitude of the

165

Crossing the plains in 1849. A wagon drawn by a four-yoke team. From a photograph of a painting (c. 1915). *Courtesy, Library of Congress.*

forty-niners. "On the last day of April, 1849, we began our journey to California," Mrs. Royce's diary begins. "Our outfit consisted of a covered wagon, well-loaded with provisions, and such preparations for sleeping, cooking, etc. as we had been able to furnish, guided only by the light of Frémont's *Travels*, and the suggestions, often conflicting, of the many who, like ourselves, utter strangers to camping life, were setting out for the 'Golden Gate.' Our wagon was drawn by three yoke of oxen and one yoke of cows, the latter being used in the team only part of the time. Their milk was of course to be a valuable part of our subsistence." The Royces followed a route that took them by Council Bluffs, Salt Lake City, Carson Desert, and over the mountains to Hangtown (Placerville), California. Along the way they were joined by other wagons until they had a sufficient train for mutual protection.

Their trail was well worn by previous immigrants. Sometimes they passed grim reminders of tragedy: graves of men, women, or children who had died; the skeletons of horses and cattle; broken wagons; and wrecked furniture. In some places, earlier droves of cattle and horses had eaten all the grass, and forage was hard to find. Worse still, rumors of an epidemic of cholera reached the Royces, and an old man, who had joined them, took sick in the Royces' wagon and died of the disease. Crossing the Carson Desert,

166

they came near death from thirst. When at long last they reached the eastern slopes of the Sierras, the season was too far advanced to get wagons through the snow-choked passes. Abandoning their wagon, the Royces obtained two mules from government agents patrolling the mountains to aid stranded immigrants, and on these mounts they made their way over the mountains to the goldfields. With only the saddlebags of a mule to hold her necessities, Mrs. Royce nevertheless found space for a Bible and a copy of John Milton's poems.

The great migration to California, inspired by a kind of insane frenzy for gold, sent thousands across the seas and overland to the West Coast in the two years after the news of the gold strike spread abroad. "During the first week of February, 1849," Cleland asserted, "fifty vessels sailed from American ports for San Francisco. By the middle of March 17,000 persons had taken passage from cities on the Gulf and Atlantic coasts; and before the year closed 230 American vessels reached California harbors." Besides these, vessels began arriving from Mexico, Central and South America, Australia, and other foreign ports.

"The overland migration," Cleland continued, "when it began, was even larger than that which came by sea. Within three weeks, during the spring of 1849, nearly 18,000 persons crossed the Missouri River for California. A single observer counted eleven hundred wagons on the prairies beyond Independence. From the Missouri frontier to Fort Laramie the procession of emigrants passed in an unbroken stream for more than two months toward the West. . . . Fully 35,000 people took part in the great overland movement of 1849, a year that rightly occupies a unique place in California and national history."

On reaching California, the immigrants hurried off toward the Sacramento Valley, the streams beyond, and the foothills of the Sierras, where gold had been reported. Soon thousands of men were panning the sands of the streams, searching every pothole and rift in the rocks, and digging out earth from the hillsides which they washed in hastily rigged troughs and sluices to separate the heavy gold flakes from the lighter soil. Some struck it rich, others had only hard labor for their pains, but most found enough gold to keep them encouraged. Frequently those who profited most were men canny enough to stock goods which the miners needed. Prices, of course, were exorbitant, and no conscience kept profiteers from charging all the traffic would bear. At the mines, one contemporary writer reported, potatoes sold for 25 cents a pound, milk brought $2 a gallon, and other foodstuffs were in proportion. But, he added, if a man was making $16 a day panning gold, he could afford the high prices. Sometimes prices were much higher. One adventurer, E. Gould Buffum, who wrote *Six Months in the Gold Fields* (1850), reported that at a camp near Coloma, he and a companion stopped to get food for breakfast which consisted of "one box of sardines, one pound of sea-biscuit, one pound of butter, a half-pound of cheese, and two bottles of ale." Their bill was $43. He had previously tried to buy a coarse work shirt, but the price was $16.

Gold was used as a medium of exchange, and every merchant and every bank had scales for weighing it. The time when the sale of gold would be restricted by the government was still far distant. Banks readily took gold dust and nuggets and exchanged them for coins; the legal rate was $20.67 per troy ounce. Twelve troy ounces made a pound. In the diggings, individuals frequently used gold as the medium of exchange, rather than bother to go to a bank to change it for currency.

The first mining was the work of amateurs, who knew nothing of engineering or scientific techniques of separating precious metals from ore. The gold they sought was loose gold in the sands of the rivers and soil of the canyons and hillsides. Anyone with a strong back, the ability to wield pick and shovel, and wit enough to pour water in a trough could hope to find gold shining at the bottom when the lighter debris had washed away. After the first few years, when free-lance miners had dug over enormous areas, large-scale scientific mining began. Crushing mills were installed to grind the gold-bearing quartz found in rocky seams in the hillsides, and the fortunes of individual prospectors waned.

The thrill of the first discovery of gold was reported by Buffum in a passage describing his own experience near Weaver's Creek:

I had slung pick, shovel and bar upon my shoulder, and trudged merrily away to a ravine about a mile from our house. Pick, shovel, and bar did their duty, and I soon had a large rock in view. Getting down into the excavation I had made, and seating myself upon the rock, I commenced a careful search for a crevice, and at last found one extending longitudinally along the rock. It appeared to be filled with a hard bluish clay and gravel, which I took out with my knife, and there at the bottom, strewn along the whole length of the rock, was bright, yellow gold, in little pieces about the size and shape of a grain of barley. . . . I scooped it out with the point of my knife and an iron spoon, and placing it in my pan, ran home with it very much delighted. I weighed it and found that my first day's labor in the mines had made me thirty-one dollars richer than I was in the morning.

Other miners were luckier, Buffum stated. "John Sullivan, an Irishman, who, when I first arrived at San Francisco, was driving an ox-team, sometime in the summer of 1848 discovered a canyon near the Stanislaus River, which proved so rich that ere the winter was over he had taken twenty-six thousand dollars worth of gold dust." Another man, one of Buffum's companions named Stockton, discovered that trade with the Indians for gold they had found was more profitable than digging himself, for he "sold several boxes of raisins to the Indians at their weight in gold." Some of the prospectors whom Buffum encountered found great lumps of gold. "The largest piece of gold which has yet been found was picked up in a dry ravine near the Stanislaus River in September 1848. It contained a large admixture of quartz, and weighed a little over twenty-five pounds, being worth five thousand dollars. A piece weighing twenty-seven ounces and a half was found by a young man named Taylor at Kelsey's Dry Diggings on the South Fork, about eight miles from Coloma. I saw this piece at the mill last spring." Reports like Buffum's, printed and circulated in the East, continued to raise the temperature of the gold fever and stirred thousands more to set out for California.

The population of California, exclusive of Indians, at the end of 1848 has been estimated at approximately 20,000. A year later it had increased to something approaching 100,000. By late 1852 the population had increased to 223,000. About one-fourth of these newcomers were not from the States. Early in the gold rush many Chileans, Peruvians, and Mexicans had come to the goldfields. The most unsavory and troublesome characters were former British convicts who had served out their terms in the penal colony in Australia. From Germany, France, and Great Britain came prospectors and adventurers. The Chinese also heard of the riches of California, and by 1852 California had 25,000 Chinese, most of whom took to the hills in search of gold.

California was admitted as a state of the Union in 1850. Before that time, it had been a territory with a semblance of military government. During 1848 and 1849 miners in the wilderness knew only such laws as they made themselves. Committees at a camp would get together to decide about the extent of a mining district, the amount of territory one man could claim (or stake out), the sort of notice required to stake a claim, penalties for the infringement of rights, and punishment for wrongdoing of various sorts.

The first towns in the goldfields usually would boast of

only two or three wooden buildings, and most of the "houses" were canvas tents, sometimes with a wooden floor but often with nothing but dirt below. Since such habitations could not be secured with lock and key, the miners sought to discourage thievery by summary punishment of malefactors. When caught, a thief might be tried by a hastily collected jury and immediately whipped or, in some cases, hanged. A contemporary writer, A. Delano, in *Life on the Plains and Among the Diggings* (1854), recounted the type of quick justice meted out: "While I was in Marysville in March, 1850, a cloth house was cut open with a knife and a trunk stolen containing $1,000. The thieves were arrested as they were preparing to go down to the river, taken before the alcalde [mayor], and sentenced to be whipped. . . . About the same time two men in Placer County went into a tent and finding a woman alone, her husband being out at work, bound and gagged her, and then robbed the tent of fifteen hundred dollars. The thieves were arrested, and as there were no prisons in

Vigilance court in session. From an engraving after a drawing by Frenzeny and Tavernier, in *Harper's Weekly* (April 11, 1874).

the country, they were whipped and again turned loose." We can be certain that the whippings were severe, but these thieves were luckier than others who were summarily executed.

Lawlessness and the ineffectiveness of any form of law enforcement, even in such populated places as San Francisco, led to the formation of groups of substantial citizens into vigilance committees, which took the law into their own hands in an effort to stamp out thievery, arson, and murder. A climax of indignation was reached in San Francisco in February, 1851, when two former convicts from Australia beat up and robbed a merchant. The indignation of the citizens was increased because this was the culmination of many crimes of violence; previously criminals had been freed by corrupt officials on some quibble of the law. Now the leading citizens of San Francisco got together to wipe out violence. They appointed a jury of twelve, tried the two robbers, and hanged them forthwith. Another instance was described by Delano: "On the night of the 11th [of June, 1851] a man named Jenkins, a Sydney convict, was taken in the act of robbing a safe. A jury was selected, indubitable proof of his guilt was adduced, and he was hung immediately, about two o'clock in the morning."

This summary justice was approved by the best citizens, and it soon rid San Francisco of the worst of its lawlessness, Delano asserted:

From this time the Vigilance Committee held sway, and their ranks were swelled by a voluntary enrollment of great numbers of the best and most effective citizens, and although opposition was offered at various times by those in authority, and by interested lawyers who were losing a fruitful source of revenue in the defence of scoundrels, they maintained their ground and within ten days the good effects of their administration was seen and felt. An effective and active police was thus formed, the rogues were

172

either caught or banished, and the city was relieved from the thralldom of their presence.

The first flush of success in the goldfields, when almost anybody could find enough of the previous metal to repay his labor, lured many physically unfit and inexperienced men into the mountains. Sickness overtook many of these, and they died miserably, often with only a thin blanket on the cold earth for a bed and perhaps a bit of canvas stretched over a tree limb to serve as a tent. The winter of 1849–50 was one of the wettest on record in California. Torrential rains fell for weeks on end; the Sacramento River and all its tributaries rose in flood, and the valleys were reduced to lakes and quagmires. Cattle drowned by the thousands. Men were often marooned in the mountains for weeks; some perished for lack of proper food, and others drowned in the swollen streams. Homesick and weary, unable to search for the gold that had lured them to California, many miners who lived through the dismal winter bitterly regretted ever leaving their homes in the East. On the way out they had sung:

> Oh Susanna, don't you cry for me,
> I'm off to California with a washbowl on my knee
> Oh California! that's the land for me!
> I'm bound for Sacramento
> With the washbowl on my knee.

Now some of the miners changed the refrain to a sour parody of their marching song:

> Oh California! this is the land for me;
> A pick and shovel, and lots of bones,
> Who would not come the sight to see—
> The golden land of dross and stones.
> Oh Susanna, don't you cry for me
> I am living dead in Californee.

Sacramento as it was in December, 1849. From a lithograph by
W. Endicott & Co. after a drawing by C. V. Cooper. *Courtesy,
Library of Congress.*

The intense competition in the goldfields, the need for
more technical methods of mining, and the requirement
of more capital than most free-lancers could raise gradually forced out of the goldfields many of the immigrants
who had swarmed into California. They drifted from one
occupation to another. Many ran "hotels"—often miserable
huts under canvas—others set up as storekeepers selling
supplies needed by the miners. Indeed, in these early days,
more California fortunes were founded on profits from
merchandising than on gold dug from the mines.

An example of a merchant who saw an opportunity and
profited thereby was Levi Strauss, who manufactured bib-
less blue denim overalls, reinforced at points of stress with
copper rivets. These overalls were exceedingly popular
and came to be the uniform of workers in the West. In
time the trademark Levis became a synonym for blue
denim pants, and the name has stuck until the present
day.

Miners had reason to bless Levi Strauss and Company,
for durable clothing was hard to find in California. Soon
everybody was wearing Strauss' blue denim overalls,
along with a woolen shirt, red, blue, or maybe striped.

That outfit, plus a bandanna around the neck, was the characteristic work dress of Californians.

Towns developed in California with amazing rapidity. From a wilderness of tents, brush huts, and shacks, order and form at length emerged, as sawmills supplied boards and timbers for more substantial structures. San Francisco, the main port of entry, grew faster than the rest. Large wooden hotels, an infinite number of saloons and less savory resorts, a theater, churches, and substantial residences soon lined the streets. Since wood was the principal structural material, San Francisco and other California towns had frequent disastrous fires.

Every town and mining camp had its quota of saloons and gambling resorts. Indeed, gambling was the chief vice of Californians in this era. Sunday was a gala day, when miners quit work and came to town. Some puritanical observers who visited the goldfields were horrified at the goings-on and wrote about roaring orgies in a way to make the mining towns sound like Western versions of Sodom and Gomorrah.

But not all miners were drunkards and gamblers. Many sober and God-fearing men had come to the goldfields. They thriftily saved the money they made and planned for the future. A large number of educated and professional men could be found among the forty-niners. Some of these brought books, and in a few towns and mining camps kindred spirits organized literary clubs and debating societies. Cultivation and a civilized way of life would not be allowed to die even in the roughest wilderness camp.

While she and her husband were living in the little mining town of Grass Valley, Mrs. Royce noted in her diary an encounter with a young man, who stopped to speak to her and her little daughter, Mary, because the child reminded the homesick youth of his sister back home. "He proved to be a young physician who had not long com-

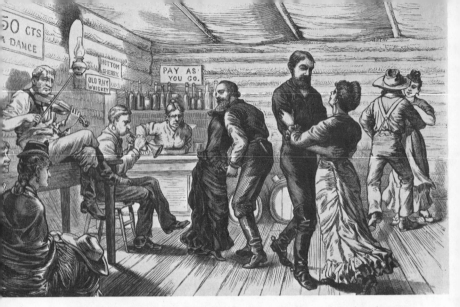

A dance house in the mining town of Leadville, Colorado—the New Eldorado. From a wood engraving in *Leslie's Illustrated* (May 24, 1879). *Courtesy, Library of Congress.*

menced to practice at home when the news of the gold discovery in California induced him to seek El Dorado. . . . His partner in work was a well educated lawyer; and another of their party was a scientist who had been applying his knowledge in geology and mineralogy in exploring. . . . Here, then, was a party of California miners, dressed in the usual mining attire, and carrying pick, shovel, and pans to and from their work, who yet were cultured gentlemen." Mrs. Royce herself helped maintain some of the elements of civilization by teaching children in the mining district.

Gold mining remained an important industry in California for many years, but within a decade after Marshall found gold in Sutter's millrace, the mad fever had cooled. Already some of the mines were worked out, and towns which had sprung up like mushrooms were quickly deserted to become the ghost towns of later years. Nothing like the excitement of the gold rush had ever before been seen in America. Later gold strikes, particularly those in

Colorado, Nevada, and the Yukon, would cause excitement, but no mass movement of miners equal to the California migration would again occur. Men, women, and children would continue to flow to the West in a steady stream for generations to come, but the mad frenzy was quieted, only to recur sporadically when news spread of riches to be found in some gulch in the Rockies, the mountains of Nevada, or the Black Hills of South Dakota.

Life in Gold Rush Towns (1850)

Alonzo Delano of Illinois went out to California in 1849 with a wagon train of immigrants. He took supplies sufficient to allow him to establish himself as a merchant in the mining camps. In 1854 he published *Life on the Plains and Among the Diggings* which gives vivid pictures of conditions in the West. In the passage below he tells about the rapid growth of California towns and the prevalence of gambling for high stakes among the miners.

Before returning to the mines, I visited Sacramento, and the improvements not only in the city, but in the country around, which a few months had produced, astonished me. Along the road hotels and dwellings had been erected at convenient distances; and where we had traveled the previous fall without seeing a human habitation, was now the abode of civilized man. At Nichols' Ranch, near the mouth of Bear River, where then but a single adobe house stood, a town had been laid out, and buildings were going rapidly up, (but this, however, eventually declined) and under the bank, in the river, a large brig was moored, which had doubled Cape Horn. Vernon and Fremont, at the mouth of Feather River, appeared flourishing, but subsequently shared the uncertain fate of new towns in a new country. All these may revive, as the country advances in population, and its agricultural resources are properly developed.

Sacramento City had become a city indeed. Substantial wooden buildings had taken the place of the cloth tents and frail tenements of the previous November, and, although it had been recently submerged by an unprecedented flood,

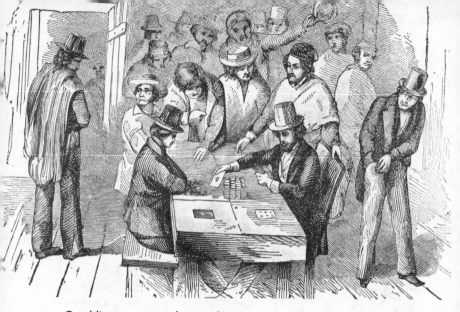

Gambling was prevalent in frontier towns. This is a scene in San Francisco during the gold rush. From a wood engraving in John Frost's *Pictorial History of California* (1850). Courtesy, Library of Congress.

which occasioned a great destruction of property, and which ruined hundreds of its citizens, it exhibited a scene of busy life and enterprise, peculiarly characteristic of the Anglo-Saxon race by whom it was peopled. An immense business was doing with miners in furnishing supplies; the river was lined with ships, the streets were thronged with drays, teams, and busy pedestrians; the stores were large, and well filled with merchandise; and even Aladdin could not have been more surprised at the power of his wonderful lamp, than I was at the mighty change which less than twelve months had wrought, since the first cloth tent had now grown into a large and flourishing city.

I regret to say, that gambling formed a prominent part in the business of the city; and there appeared an infatuation, if not unprecedented, certainly not excelled in the annals of mankind. Long halls had been erected, which were splendidly lighted, and beautifully decorated with rich pictures, having magnificent bars, where liquors and various refreshments were exhibited, to tempt a depraved appetite;

and along the center and sides of the room tables were arranged, where piles of money were seductively laid out to tempt the cupidity of the unexperienced. And to crown all, on raised forms, or finely wrought galleries, bands of music "discoursed harmonious sounds," to attract a crowd. These places of resort were daily and nightly thronged with men of all ages and conditions in life, eager to tempt the fickle goddess of Fortune, too often to their own ruin. Large sums were freely staked, and often changed hands, and the hard earnings of the infatuated miner, which he had been months in accumulating by incessant toil and wearying hardships, frequently passed from his well-filled purse, to swell the gambler's bank that was spread seductively, before him.

A day or two previous to my arrival, I was told that a young man, having started for home, came to the city from the mines, with nineteen thousand dollars. On his arrival he deposited sixteen thousand with a friend, and with the rest went into one of these splendid hells, and commenced betting at monte. He soon lost this, and under the excitement which it occasioned, he drew the sixteen thousand from his friend, notwithstanding all remonstrance, and determined to retrieve his luck. He returned to the table, and continued playing till he had lost every farthing, when, instead of making his friends happy, by returning to their embrace with a competence, he was compelled to return to toil and privation in the mines. Another, with fifteen hundred dollars, began playing, with the avowed intention of breaking the bank; but the result was, as might have been anticipated, the gambler won every dollar in a short time. With the utmost coolness the poor fool observed to the banker, "You have won all my money—give me an ounce to get back to the mines with." Without saying a word, the gambler handed him back sixteen dollars, and the victim returned to his toil again.

Even boys of twelve and sixteen years of age were sometimes seen betting. But little else could be expected, from the extent of the demoralizing influences thus set before them.

In passing down to Sacramento through some of the

mining settlements, I could not but observe the march of refinement which was going on, or, more properly speaking, the comforts, which were introduced. Crockery and tablecloths appeared on the tables of the hotels along the road; glass tumblers, and even wine glasses, were used; berths, similar to those on steamboats, were made around the rooms, and occasionally spare blankets could be found, so that on the principal thoroughfares it was no longer necessary to sleep on the ground, nor carry one's own plate, knife, and tin cup; and as early as July, 1850, a line of stages commenced running from Sacramento to Marysville, which the following year became a very important and well-regulated route, from which, in 1851, lines diverged to various points in the mines.

During the winter of 1849 and '50, one of the greatest floods occurred which had ever been known in the valley of the Sacramento. From the top of a high hill on the left bank of Feather River, not far from the Table Mountain, where I could command an extensive view of the valley, I estimated that one-third of the land was overflowed. Hundreds of cattle, horses and mules were drowned, being carried down by the rapidity of the current in their attempt to reach higher ground; and Sacramento City, then being without its levee, was almost entirely submerged. A small steamboat actually run [sic] up its principal streets, and discharged its freight on the steps of one of the principal stores (Starr, Bensley & Co.'s).

7

Ranchers and Homesteaders
in the Great West

ALTHOUGH the gold fever diminished in intensity as
mining grew more difficult and less profitable, the infection
did not die out. From time to time, with the news of gold
strikes in some distant part of the West, the old excitement
flared again and sent flocks of miners trooping in search
of rich bonanzas. The mining craze was responsible for
opening up parts of Nevada, Colorado, Idaho, South Dakota, and other areas that otherwise would have remained
of interest only to Indians and occasional trappers. No part
of the United States was unaffected by the lure of the
mines. From New England to the Deep South, men
packed up their belongings and headed West. Nowhere,
however, was the restlessness greater than in the newly
settled regions west of the Mississippi River. Every rumor of
wealth to be dug from the earth excited people living in
this frontier zone. Americans have always been characterized by a readiness to pick up and move, an eagerness to
try their fortunes in some new place. From the mid-nineteenth century onward, this restlessness resulted in a shifting population that ultimately served to fill up the open

Prospectors and emigrants en route to Leadville. Note dead animals along the trail. From *Leslie's* (May 24, 1879).

spaces of the West. And in this movement, miners and would-be miners led the procession.

During the summer and autumn of 1858 newspapers in Missouri began to print stories of gold strikes in Colorado near the present site of Denver. Before winter set in, trails leading to the Colorado mountains were swarming with prospectors. Covered wagons clogged the roads, and many of them proclaimed their destination with crudely lettered signs reading; *Pikes Peak Or Bust.* A printer, with a canny eye on the market, brought out the *Pikes Peak Guide,* which quickly became a best seller. Many of the prospectors, who reached the mountains as winter began, nearly froze before the coming of spring. But by the time the ice melted, fresh hordes swarmed into the hills. Before the year was out, more than 100,000 prospectors had tramped over the Colorado mountains, but most of them found no gold and returned to their homes in the East poorer than they came. A few, however, discovered veins of profitable ore and in time developed gold and silver mines that brought prosperity to Denver, Boulder, Leadville, Central City, Cripple Creek, and other spots whose names are now associated with the romance of mining in Colorado.

About the time miners were swarming into Colorado,

they also began to prospect the eastern slope of the Sierras in Nevada, and in gulches on the side of Davidson Mountain they struck gold mixed with a black substance that turned out to be silver. One miner named Henry Comstock found an especially rich vein, known in mining history as the Comstock Lode. The gold and silver of Davidson Mountain and its canyons attracted thousands of miners. They built Virginia City into a roaring mining camp described by Mark Twain in *Roughing It*. It is now a ghost town and a tourist attraction.

Mining in Virginia City was not an occupation for adventurous individuals with shovel and pan; free-lance mining gave way to a new type requiring capital and machinery, but eager investors were ready to back almost

The Corduroy Road over the Rockies to Leadville. From a wood engraving after E. Jump, in *Leslie's* (1879).

Coming down the Sierra Nevadas, 1865. From a wood engraving in A. D. Richardson, *Beyond the Mississippi* (1867).

A stagecoach leaving the International Hotel, Virginia City, Nevada, for California. From a photograph (n.d.) in the collections of the Library of Congress.

A gambling hall in Denver City, Colorado. From a wood engraving after a sketch by T. R. Davis, in *Harper's Weekly* (February 17, 1766).

any project. One group, deciding that the Comstock Lode could be tapped deep within the earth, sank a shaft and hit a vein so rich that in time it produced $200,000,000. The wealth from this vein, called the Big Bonanza, stimulated efforts by other companies to discover bonanzas equally rich.

No scheme was too fantastic to find investors willing to take a chance. Although free-lance miners no longer could hope to make a fortune panning gold, prospectors believed they might find a vein of ore and sell their claims for a fortune. Speculation in mining rights became an industry in itself, and the sale of bogus mines was one of the biggest frauds of the day. The smell of quick riches always attracts the least desirable of humankind, and the mines of Colorado and Nevada soon drew flocks of speculators, gamblers, shysters, women of shady reputation, and almost any type of crook known in the annals of crime. When lawlessness grew too rampant, the mining towns sometimes invoked vigilante justice, gave criminals an impromptu trial, and strung them up to the nearest tree.

Each new mining frontier reenacted the history, with slight variations, of preceding mining regions. The discovery of gold and silver in Idaho, Montana, and South Dakota brought swarms of prospectors and miners into those regions. It made little difference that land there belonged to the Indians. Nothing could hold back swarms of miners once the cry of gold was heard. Like water piling up behind a frail dam, gold miners broke all barriers and went wherever they thought they could find the precious metal.

The Civil War, raging back East from 1861 to 1865, slowed but did not stop the miners' search for gold in the West. Many a draft dodger found the goldfields of California, Nevada, and Montana more to his liking than the battlefields of Virginia. During the height of the war, in 1863, thousands of prospectors swarmed into the river valleys of Montana. Within three years miners took more than $30,000,000 in gold out of Alder Gulch and some $16,000,-000 from the environs of Helena.

Prospectors and miners were the spearheads for other immigrants, who followed them into hitherto unsettled country. The mining industry made a market for all manner of goods, as well as farm products. Merchants and traders followed the miners, and farmers and ranchers soon established themselves in regions that the miners first opened up. By the mid-nineteenth century, restless people were astir along the entire frontier, and the movement that would eventually fill up the continent was under way. Many miners who failed to find gold remained to enter business or to turn farmers. Returning adventurers told tales of the Western country that set others on fire to try their own fortunes. Every boy dreamed of adventures in the West; both young and old greedily read accounts of travelers who had visited the country of the buffalo and the Indian.

Some of the explorers of the region between the Missouri River and the Rocky Mountains, notably Zebulon

186

Pike in 1806 and Stephen H. Long in 1820, had decided that the land was unfit for agriculture. Long had labeled on his map a vast territory as the Great American Desert. Gradually, however, travelers refuted this notion of one endless desert.

One daring character who was not frightened at the thought of the Great American Desert was Brigham Young, leader of the Church of Jesus Christ of Latter-day Saints, popularly known as the Mormons, a sect founded by Joseph Smith in 1830 in upper New York State. It was Young who welded the Mormons into a coherent group after Smith's death and led them into the wilderness to make a garden spot out of Utah.

The Mormons had good reason to seek a refuge out of reach of other religionists, for they had already suffered much persecution. Driven from New York to Ohio, to Missouri, and eventually to Illinois, where they had created a thriving city at Nauvoo, they could not escape their enemies. Their clannish ways and Smith's prophecy that the Saints would eventually rule the earth created suspicion in each community where they settled. Finally, Smith's claim to a divine revelation condoning polygamy for the leaders of the faithful resulted in a violent reaction against the Mormons. Puritanical folk everywhere condemned them as anti-Christian. Finally, on June 27, 1844, Smith and his brother were lynched by a mob in Carthage, Illinois. Feeling against the Mormons was so intense that only the promise of the leaders that they would leave Illinois prevented riots that would have amounted to civil war. The man who took command at this critical time was Brigham Young, an executive and administrator of genius. Rarely has any colonial enterprise been planned with such skill, intelligence, and wisdom as was the colonization of the Mormon state in the valley of the Great Salt Lake.

The population of Nauvoo, the Mormon metropolis in Illinois, numbered something more than 16,000 souls. Young planned their evacuation by stages. The first group

Brigham Young, leader of the Mormons—a portrait made in his later years. From an engraving by H. B. Hall & Sons (n.d.). *Courtesy, Library of Congress.*

moved out in the late winter of 1846 and settled in a camp at Sugar Grove, Iowa. During the late winter and spring the rest of the population moved across the Mississippi River and set up temporary quarters in Iowa camps. Anti-Mormon mobs and drunken rowdies took possession of Nauvoo, drove out the few old and sickly Mormons left, threw non-Mormon sympathizers in the river, and ultimately burned the temple. A large body of refugees eventually collected in a camp that Brigham Young designated Winter Quarters, on the site of modern Omaha, Nebraska, but small detachments established intermediary base camps from the Mississippi River all the way across Iowa. In accordance with Young's instructions, they planted crops and made shelters for immigrant parties to follow. Missionaries had been busy throughout the East and in Europe, especially England, and Young planned to gather the converts they had made into the New Jerusalem that he was planning. For years to come, immigrants would use the trail being prepared. Corn, turnips, squash, and beans planted by one group would be gathered and used for food by succeeding parties, who would replant when the season permitted so that others who followed would find supplies.

To ensure peace with the Indians, Young made a treaty with Big Elk, chief of the Omahas. In return for the help of Mormon blacksmiths in repairing the Indians' weapons and implements, Big Elk promised that his young men would guard the immigrants' cattle and warn them of hostile Indians. The Omahas themselves stood in peril from the warlike Sioux and welcomed the aid of white men.

All during the summer of 1846 bands of Mormons streamed across Iowa toward Winter Quarters, and by autumn more than 12,000 were temporarily established there. Meanwhile, the Mexican War had begun, and United States Army officers asked Young to provide a company of men to march against the Mexicans in California. Although he was not enthusiastic about this venture, Young realized that some advantages might accrue from having a group of the faithful equipped and trained by the United States Army; consequently, he furnished the famous Mormon Battalion, numbering 549 men, who marched from Nebraska to San Diego, which they reached in January, 1847.

Brigham Young's first detachment of settlers to head for the unknown West left Winter Quarters in mid-April, 1847. This Pioneer Band, led by Young, consisted of 146 picked men and women. They drove livestock ahead of them and

Big Elk, whose Indian name was *Om-pah-ton-ga*. From the portrait in Catlin's Indian Gallery. *Courtesy, Smithsonian Institution.*

Part of the Mormon camp at Fort Bridger, Utah Territory. From a wood engraving in *Harper's Weekly* (January 30, 1858).

in a train of seventy-three wagons they carried tools and supplies sufficient to enable them to establish permanent homes. Blazing a trail along the north side of the Platte River to avoid rowdies headed for Oregon on the well-marked Oregon Trail south of the Platte, Young took a course that led him past Fort Laramie, South Pass, and Fort Bridger (a post operated by a famous mountain man, Jim Bridger, 100 miles east of the Great Salt Lake). The trail finally led through a ravine now known as Emigration Canyon, and the band emerged in sight of the great basin of Salt Lake. Young looked out across the expanse before him and said, "This is the place."

Not all his followers were convinced that their leader had discovered paradise. The sight before them appeared unpromising to some of the less imaginative and less determined. One man complained that the land showed only a scanty growth even of sagebrush and greasewood. But living streams emptied into the Great Salt Lake, and along their borders willows and aspens grew, and grass abounded in the meadows. Young knew that he could make something of the recalcitrant land; furthermore, he hoped that its outward barrenness would discourage greedy Gentiles (the name given non-Mormons) from following the Saints. He believed that he was outside the borders of the United States. He could not foresee that a year later Mexico would cede all the West to the victorious United States.

The Pioneer Band, under Young's direction, immediately set to work to subdue the desert. They dug canals, turned water on the thirsty soil, and planted grain and potatoes. The Mormons were the first settlers in the West to irrigate land on a large scale, and their irrigation projects became a model for others to follow. After food crops had been planted, Young ordered the Pioneer Band to lay out a city in neat squares. Here would be the center of a Mormon society that would flourish, he hoped, undisturbed by outside influences.

From Winter Quarters, from Eastern cities, and from Europe, Mormons during the next few years poured into the great basin of Salt Lake. Many settled in Salt Lake City, but others founded towns on the rivers and streams of the region. Within a few years the state of Deseret, as the Mormons called their land, was a flourishing domain ruled over by Brigham Young, who supervised every detail of the lives of his people. To ensure that they established a self-sufficient agricultural community, he ordained that the Saints should not engage in mining. Too many frontier communities, he knew, had been deserted when the populace got wind of a gold strike somewhere else. He was taking no chance of his people's flocking to California or Nevada in search of gold dust. It would be better for them to grow corn, wheat, turnips, and potatoes in Utah, a name the United States government gave this territory. People had to eat. Furthermore, Young soon had sawmills

"This is the place." The first view of Great Salt Lake, from Emigration Canyon. From a lithograph by Ackerman, in H. Stansbury, *An Expedition to the Valley of the Great Salt Lake* (1852).

operating on streams in the hills, and he encouraged his people to open tanneries, leatherworks, wagon shops, and other industries that would free them of dependence on imports from the East. As soon as sheep multiplied sufficiently to supply wool, Young opened a woolen mill.

Life was not easy, but the Mormons surmounted every obstacle. To divine intervention they credited their salvation in the early days of settlement, when swarms of crickets threatened to destroy their crops. In the nick of time, flocks of seagulls arrived to eat up the crickets. But hard work, careful planning, ingenuity, and singleness of purpose accounted for the Mormons' success in bringing prosperity to the settlements of Utah.

These people were not above driving a hard bargain at the expense of Gentile immigrants who passed through their territory. Even when the Pioneer Band was on the way West, Young saw an opportunity to make a profit from the Gentiles. To get his supplies over the rain-swollen Platte, he rigged up a ferry. When a party of immigrants headed for Oregon turned up at the river, Young agreed to ferry them across at a charge of $15 per wagon, payable in flour at $2.50 per hundredweight, which the Mormons could sell at Fort Laramie for four times that price. Hauling Gentiles over the Platte proved so profitable that Young kept a party of stout ferrymen busy so long as the high water lasted. Later, at other points in Mormon territory, travelers complained that the settlers poured water in mudholes and charged exorbitant fees for pulling out Gentile wagons that got stuck.

The Mormon religion emphasized hard work, thrift, and neighborliness to members of the faith. Mutual helpfulness was a tenet of other frontier folk but was particularly emphasized by the Mormons. They also believed that religion should make them a happy people. The kind of sour Puritanism that had characterized seventeenth-century New England was an anathema to the Mormons, as were some of the prohibitions of other religions. For example, the Meth-

Crossing a tributary of the Platte on an improvised ferry similar to the one used by Mormon pioneers. From a lithograph by Ackerman (1851). *Courtesy, Library of Congress.*

odists condemned dancing, but the Mormons found Scriptural justification for dancing and gaiety. Dancing, music, and frolics which brought together all the people, old and young, became part of their religious practice.

Young insisted that education was also essential to a happy and successful people, and he established schools, ordered textbooks printed, and encouraged literary and debating societies. Amateur theatricals were common, and more than one Mormon community saw its young people acting in Shakespeare's plays.

The practice of polygamy, however, was one element in the Mormon creed that proved repugnant to other religionists and in the end brought the wrath of the United States government down on the Mormon commonwealth. Not every Mormon approved of this unconventional "revelation" that had come from heaven to Joseph Smith, but the practice slowly spread. Brigham Young set an example by taking a number of wives, variously estimated at from seventeen to twenty-seven, depending on the precise classification given his various unions. Some wives he took merely to give them protection and support.

A ball at the Mormon Theater, Salt Lake City. From a wood engraving in *Harper's Weekly* (October 10, 1857).

In a frontier society, which had many more women than men, plural marriage was a virtual necessity to provide the unattached women with homes and a stable position in the social order. Although the system of plural wives appears to have been a reasonably satisfactory solution of the problem of surplus women, many of them converts who had been induced to come to Utah from England and Europe, the practice gave enemies of the Mormons a high moral issue with which to attack them. Anti-Mormon writers heaped abuse on them for their alleged immorality.

When one of Brigham Young's wives, Ann Eliza Young, deserted and sued for divorce, the case became a *cause célèbre*. The publication of *Wife No. 19* (1879), purportedly a personal description of her experience in Young's harem, created a sensation. Other violent and vicious diatribes against the Mormons poured from the anti-Mormon press. As early as 1862, a law was passed by Congress outlawing polygamy in territories of the United States; this was followed by various other laws, but not until 1882 was a federal law enacted with sufficient teeth to suppress polygamy. Seeing the handwriting on the wall, the church issued a manifesto in 1890 eliminating polygamy as a practice officially approved.

Over the years the Mormons suffered continued harassment from holier-than-thou elements in American society. Gentiles in Utah and other regions into which Mormons filtered were envious of their prosperity and the methods by which they favored members of their own sect. Although Utah had been established as a territory of the United States in 1850, thus destroying Brigham Young's dream of an independent Mormon nation, the Mormons managed, often against great political odds, to maintain actual, if not nominal, control of their territory through most of its history. Not until 1896 was Utah admitted as a state. But Young and his successors had to make compromises to comport with the laws of Congress. One of the compromises was the manifesto removing polygamy from the dogma.

The accomplishments of the Mormons in creating a flourishing, prosperous, and self-sustaining society in a barren frontier region were so remarkable that they deserve special attention in any study of the development of the American frontier. Without an almost fanatical zeal to perpetuate their faith—and without a leader with the firmness and the wisdom of Brigham Young—it is doubtful whether they would have had the cohesion and ability to make so great a success.

From the beginning, the Mormons emphasized hard work as a virtue. Nobody was exempt from performing his or her share of any labor required. No feeling of indignity was attached to work with the hands. The whole family shared in the daily activities, whatever they were. At first, Utah, like all the frontier regions, was almost exclusively a farming community. Gradually, as industry and shopkeeping developed, a greater division of labor occurred, but throughout its early years nearly everybody

Chores for everybody. Every family had livestock that had to be tended. From a lithograph by L. Pranc & Co.

worked a piece of land, if nothing more than a garden. Everybody had some livestock, if no more than a horse, a milk cow or two, and poultry. That meant daily chores for the boys and girls. The boys looked after the livestock; the girls fed the chickens, took care of the milk, and did the churning. On a fully operated farm the women and girls took their turns in the fields at planting and harvest times. The men did the heavy labor of plowing, harrowing, cutting corn, reaping wheat and rye, and other backbreaking work, but women often were called on to thin the newly sprouted corn, hoe out the weeds in corn and root crops, to feed the pigs, and to perform a variety of chores when the men were too busy with other tasks, especially in the spring and early autumn. Nobody felt that any labor was beneath him, and the notion that work of any kind diminished one's prestige would have struck a Mormon— or any other frontiersman, for that matter—as an absurd affectation that would have left him aghast at the stupidity of such a view. Before a decade was past, the labor of the Mormons and the intelligence with which they applied their efforts had already made Utah richly productive,

Harvesttime chore for boys. From a wood engraving after
a drawing by Winslow Homer, in *Harper's Weekly* (December 6, 1873).

Women and girls gathering peas. From an etching by G.
Mercier after a painting by H. Roseland.

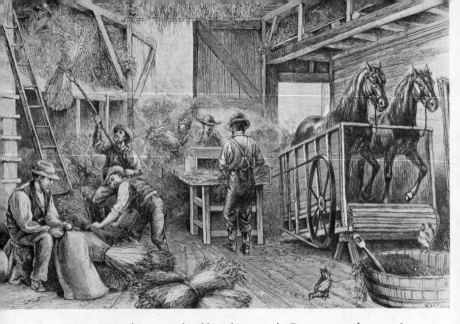

Harvesting wheat was backbreaking work. From a wood engraving in *Harper's Weekly* (August 30, 1879). Courtesy, Library of Congress.

with neat homes, well-kept gardens, orchards of fruit trees, irrigated farmlands, and spreading pasturage for cattle and sheep. Few frontiers prospered faster or gave their citizens greater satisfaction in their accomplishment.

Hostile and prejudiced as was much of the anti-Mormon writing of the mid-nineteenth century, an occasional objective account pointed out the remarkable feat of this people in conquering the desert. Such a report was made by Captain Howard Stansbury of the United States Corps of Engineers in *An Expedition to the Valley of the Great Salt Lake of Utah . . . with an Authentic Account of the Mormon Settlement* (London, 1852). "In this young and progressive country of ours," Stansbury wrote, "where cities grow up in a day and states spring into existence in a year, the successful planting of a colony where the natural advantages . . . hold out the promise of adequate reward . . . would have excited no surprise; but the success of an enterprise . . . so at variance with all . . . probability may well be considered as one of the most remarkable incidents of the present age."

Stansbury praised the constitution which the Mormons adopted before Utah became a territory; he also praised their system of justice which, he said, even Gentiles passing through Utah were glad to invoke in settling disputes. Concerning polygamy, Stansbury made observations that must have surprised prejudiced Gentiles: "Upon the practical working of this system of plurality of wives, I can hardly be expected to express more than a mere opinion," he remarked and added:

Peace, harmony, and cheerfulness seemed to prevail where my preconceived notions led me to look for nothing but the exhibition of petty jealousies, envy, bickerings, and strife. Confidence and sisterly affection among the different members of the family seemed pre-eminently conspicuous, and friendly intercourse among the neighbors, with balls, parties, and merrymakings at each others' houses formed a prominent and agreeable feature of the society. In these friendly reunions, the President [Brigham Young], with his numerous family, mingled freely, and was ever an honored and welcome guest, tempering by his presence the

Dinner at Brigham Young's. From a wood engraving in *Harper's Weekly* (1857). *Courtesy, Library of Congress.*

exuberant hilarity of the young and not unfrequently closing with devotional exercises the gaiety of a happy evening.

The rapid growth of California as a result of the gold
rush; the settlement of Utah and its growth into a prosperous farming region; the opening of productive mines in
Nevada, Colorado, Idaho, and South Dakota; the attractions of the Oregon country and the settlement of the
Willamette Valley and adjacent territory showed the need
of improved methods of transportation across the continent.

To reach California or Oregon required a long sea voyage around Cape Horn; or a voyage to Panama, a hazardous trip across the Isthmus, and another voyage northward; or a tedious and dangerous overland trip through
hostile Indian country, across parching deserts, and over
difficult mountains. Every method was slow, expensive, and
dangerous.

With the increase of immigration into the Western country, the wagon trails were better marked, way stations and
trading posts were established, and in time the Army as-
signed detachments of troops to outposts to protect, after a
fashion, wayfarers on their way West. From the time of the
opening of the Santa Fe trade out of St. Louis, wagon
trains hauling freight had regularly made trips over the
Western trails.

If the various frontier regions were to keep in touch with
civilized portions of the United States, they had to have
better methods of communication than the haphazard and
slow wagon trains that brought freight and occasional mail.
California was already in the mid-nineteenth century a
growing area, and its population wanted to get mail and
news of happenings back East. A petition signed by some
75,000 Californians in 1856 was sent to Congress begging
for the institution of regular mail service from the East.

The next year Congress voted an annual subsidy of
$600,000 to establish a mail coach line between some
point on the Mississippi River and San Francisco. This act

The overland mail—transferring passengers and mail from a stage-coach to a six-mule Celerity Wagon. From a wood engraving in *Leslie's* (October 28, 1858).

Saving the mail—a stagecoach under attack by Indians. From a photograph of a painting by Remington. *Courtesy, Library of Congress.*

The telegraph takes over from the Pony Express, 1861. From a photograph of a symbolic painting by Jackson (1936). *Courtesy, Library of Congress.*

resulted in the establishment of the famous Butterfield Overland Express, which began operating in 1858 over a devious route from St. Louis by way of Fort Smith, Arkansas; El Paso, Texas; Yuma, Arizona; San Diego and Los Angeles to San Francisco, California. Its vehicles, heavy Concord coaches made in Concord, New Hampshire, drawn by four to six horses or mules, were stout enough to stand the rough and rocky trails, but they did not promise a passenger either comfort or safety. Sometimes they crashed against boulders, turned over in some perilous pass, or were riddled by bullets from Indians or highwaymen. Nevertheless, they managed to keep a fairly regular schedule. Under their contract with the government they were obligated to make the trip and to deliver the mails within twenty-five days between St. Louis and San Francisco. Until the outbreak of the Civil War in 1861, the Butterfield Overland Express followed this route, carrying mail and passengers on a regular schedule despite the hostility of Apache and Comanche Indians along the route. Many episodes of encounters with Indians and highwaymen, later chronicled in dime novels, described attacks on the stagecoaches of the Butterfield Overland Express.

Other express routes for stagecoaches were soon established to take mail and passengers to mining districts in Colorado and Nevada. The most famous lines were those operated by Ben Holladay, who, beginning in 1862, bought out most of the other lines crossing the central part of the continent. Holladay was so famous for the speed and efficiency with which he operated his coaches that Mark Twain has a character in *Roughing It* express astonishment that Moses took forty years to get the children of Israel from Egypt to the Promised Land. Ben Holladay, he maintained, "would have fetched them through in thirty-six hours."

The effort to speed up mail delivery that appealed most to the imagination, then and later, was the establishment of the Pony Express, which operated from April 3, 1860, until October, 1861, when the opening of a transcontinental telegraph line put it out of business. But in the short time that it existed, it created excitement—and lost money for its backers, the express and shipping firm of Russell, Majors, and Waddell. The Pony Express route, from St. Joseph, Missouri, via Salt Lake City to San Francisco, established stations every 10 miles where fresh horses waited for the dashing couriers. Riding at breakneck speed, fast enough to outrun Indians or highwaymen, the boy riders usually got through the 75-mile stint that each was expected to cover. Every daredevil boy in the country wanted to be a Pony Express rider; astronauts today enjoy no more prestige than was the reward of youths chosen to carry the mails between St. Joseph and San Francisco.

Pony Express, stagecoach lines, and wagon freighters at last gave way to railways that were slowly creeping across the continent from the 1850's to the 1870's. Before the Civil War, plans were already afoot for the construction of a transcontinental railway that would join the Atlantic and

Pacific oceans. The dream that Jefferson had of a waterway across the continent had long since vanished, but now a ribbon of rails would supply an even faster method of transportation.

The plans on paper for a transcontinental railway looked simpler than actual construction proved to be. To sweeten the prospect for investors, Congress passed an act that provided long-term loans to the builders. They could get $16,000 a mile for level land, $32,000 a mile for the foothills, and $48,000 a mile for a mountain terrain. The maps that the railway promoters drew up showed an astonishing lot of mountains. The government also offered the railways a free right-of-way across government land, plus ten sections of land, each section containing 640 acres, for each mile of track laid. The land would not be continuous but would be dispersed, checkerboard fashion, along the right-of-way. Although much of this land was desert, the railroads thus obtained vast acreages, which in time enriched

Grading the Central Pacific Railroad with mule power—the cut at Owl Gap, California. From a photograph in *Gems of California Scenery* (1866). *Courtesy, Library of Congress.*

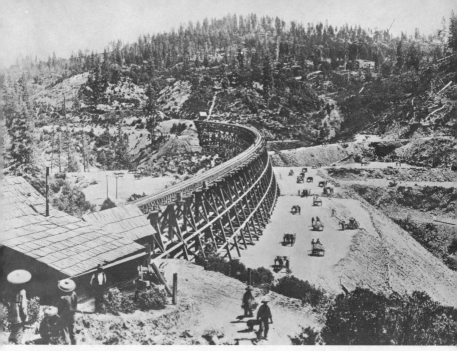

A railroad trestle being built by Chinese coolies in the Sierra Nevadas, 1877. From a photograph. *Courtesy, Southern Pacific Railway Co.*

Railroad laborers on a handcar attacked by Indians. From a wood engraving in *Leslie's* (March 26, 1870).

them. With incentives like these, promoters hurried to organize companies and start building.

On the Pacific coast, Leland Stanford, Collis P. Huntington, Mark Hopkins, and Charles Crocker (known in California history as the Big Four) organized the Central Pacific Railroad Company in 1862 and the next year started building east from Sacramento.

Meanwhile, the Union Pacific Company started westward from Omaha. Slowly the lines crept across the land. The Central Pacific, short of labor, imported thousands of Chinese coolies to grade the roadbeds. No great earthmoving equipment was then available. The grading was done with mules and drag pans, picks, shovels, and wheelbarrows. Bridges had to be built over terrifying canyons and rivers, and tunnels had to be burrowed and blasted through the Sierra Nevadas and the Rockies. How many Chinese and other workers lost their lives as the dangerous work progressed, nobody knows.

The Union Pacific had somewhat easier terrain, but its workers, composed largely of Irish immigrants, were harassed by marauding Sioux and Comanches and sometimes by great herds of buffalo stampeding across the right-of-way. Armed guards kept watch for Indians while the track beds were graded, ravines filled with earth, and tracks laid.

At long last, crews of the two companies were in sight of each other at a point in Utah called Promontory, northwest of the modern city of Ogden. On May 10, 1869, they joined the tracks. Officials from both East and West had come for the celebration. As a symbol of the importance of the event, the last spike to be driven was golden, at least gilded; but champagne flowed that day like water, and some reporters alleged that the officials given the honor of driving the golden spike had trouble hitting it.

At any rate, now at last one could cross the continent by rapid transit, at least rapid in terms of that age. Before many years passed, other rail lines were spanning the country from east to west and from north to south. By the 1880's

Buffalo stampeding across the tracks of the Kansas-Pacific Railroad.
From a wood engraving after Berghaus, in *Leslie's* (June 3, 1871).

The driving of the golden spike at Promontory Point, Utah, May 10,
1869. From a photograph of a painting by T. Hill. *Courtesy, Union
Pacific Railway.*

Loading cotton aboard a steamboat on the lower Mississippi. From a Currier & Ives lithograph in the collections of the Library of Congress.

the country was better served by rail transportation than it is today. The railroads had taken over.

The multiplication of railroads in the next two decades changed the aspect of life on the Mississippi and Missouri rivers that had been familiar to frontiersmen since the first keelboat floated down to New Orleans. In the mid-nineteenth century, steamboats on the Mississippi had provided not only reasonably rapid transportation, but they had been a source of adventure and romance. One has only to read Mark Twain's *Life on the Mississippi* to see what passage on one of the majestic river steamers meant to a traveler in that day. Fortunes were lost betting on races between some of the famous side-wheelers. Sometimes lives were also lost when stokers piled on too much rosin and pine knots and the boilers blew up.

But by the 1880's the railways had sent the steamboats into eclipse. Mark Twain, on a steamer trip on the upper river in 1882, described "the unholy train [which] comes tearing along . . . ripping the sacred solitude to rags and tatters with its devil's war-whoop and the roar and thunder of its rushing wheels. . . . This locomotive is in sight from the deck of the steamboat almost the whole way from St. Louis to St. Paul—eight hundred miles. These railroads have made havoc with the steamboat commerce," he sorrowfully observed.

In the development of the remaining frontier and in the filling up of immense areas of vacant land, the railroads played an important part. Now immigrants could reach any part of the United States with less danger and difficulty than before. They might have to endure as great hardship as their predecessors, once they reached prairie homesteads in the unsettled parts of the country, but they suffered fewer hardships in getting there.

The railroads engaged in systematic advertising campaigns in the United States and in Europe to persuade immigrants to come West. At first the railroads retained the landholdings they had obtained from the government, but at length they sold some of their vast acreages to settlers.

Fortunes were won and lost betting on steamboat races on the Mississippi. From a lithograph by A. Weingartner, after a painting by F. Fuller (1859). *Courtesy, Library of Congress.*

Scene on the Missouri River before the coming of the railroads. From an engraving in Dana, *U.S. Illustrated.*

But the majority of immigrants into the prairie country of Iowa, Nebraska, Kansas, the Dakotas, and other Western territories took up government land as homesteaders.

The question of the disposition of Western land had troubled the government from early times. Much of the land, of course, belonged to the Indians, but there was no clear demarcation of which territory belonged to which Indians. Not even the Indians themselves could agree. After the cession of the Mexican provinces in the West to the United States in 1848, the federal government assumed the ownership of Western land not in actual possession of previous owners. What the government would do with these lands was a problem that vexed politicians. A society in Ohio as early as 1812 had presented a memorial to Congress stating that "every man [is] entitled by nature to a portion of the soil of the country." During the mid-nineteenth century the notion gained further currency that man by natural law had a right to vacant land, and agitation developed for a law granting settlers the right to take up public land in the West.

Finally, in 1862, after much debate, Congress enacted the Homestead Law, which provided that "any person who is the head of a family, or who has arrived at the age of twenty-one years of age, and is a citizen of the United States, or who shall have filed his declaration of intention to become such" had the privilege of taking up a quarter section of land (160 acres) without payment, provided he lived on it for five years, cultivated a portion of it, and made some "improvements"—meaning some sort of housing. This law opened up enormous tracts of government land merely for the taking and induced many settlers to come West and homestead.

As homesteaders began to pour West, the Indian problem became acute, because many immigrants settled on lands that the Indians rightly regarded as their hunting grounds. The forty-niners headed for California and immigrants bound for Oregon had observed that the Great American Desert that Pike and Long had marked on their maps was less desolate than these explorers had indicated. Instead, here stretched endless miles of prairie land, much of it now in the states of Nebraska and Kansas, which would make good farms. Only buffalo and heathen Indians roamed this great expanse, which God surely intended Christians to occupy. So went the argument of farmers who had seen or

Rush for free land under the Homestead Law—opening of the Cherokee Strip, September 16, 1893. From a reproduction of a sketch by H. Worrall, in *Harper's Weekly* (1983). Courtesy, Library of Congress.

The Indian menace in Nebraska—a band of Sioux in ambush preparing to attack settlers. From a wood engraving after Cary, in *Harper's Weekly* (May 2, 1868).

heard about rich soil which they coveted. As the pressure of immigrants in the West increased, encroachment on Indian land caused trouble. Sometimes the federal government was able to purchase by treaty the Indians' rights, sometimes by sharp practice drunken chiefs were persuaded to cede lands and agree to move to reservations, but frequently war with the Indians resulted. The three decades after the Civil War were years of turmoil in the Indian country. At last the cavalry drove the Blackfeet, the Sioux, the Crows, the Cheyennes, the Nez Percés, the Kiowa, the Comanches, the Apaches, and other tribes to reservations. When farmers, cattlemen, and miners later began to yearn for portions of these reservations, reasons could be found for limiting still further the land allotted to the Indians. The story of our dealings with the Indians during these years in not a happy one, nor is our record always honorable. An account of the Indian wars that resulted falls outside the scope of this narrative, but suffice it to say that settlers on all the Western frontiers often stood in peril from Indians who felt that these interlopers had taken their land and destroyed their game, principally the buffalo.

When the first settlers began crossing the plains in 1848 and 1849, herds of buffalo numbering countless thousands grazed on the tall grass and at times went thundering over the landscape like an immense black cloud. An Army officer in 1886 estimated 100,000,000 buffalo in the region that now comprises Oklahoma and Kansas. How many more grazed over the rest of the Great Plains baffles the imagination.

The buffalo was essential to the life of the Western Indians. From the buffalo came skins for clothing, robes for sleeping, skins for tepees, meat for food, fats for ointments, glue for bows and arrows, horns for implements and utensils, rib bones for use where wooden staves could not be found, and dried dung (buffalo "chips") used as fuel for cooking and warmth. The buffalo was the complete "commissary" or "market" for the Indian. He hunted the buffalo in various ways: by stamped-

U.S. Cavalry vs. Indians. From a photograph of a painting by Schreyvogel. *Courtesy, Library of Congress.*

Indian women dressing buffalo skins in a Comanche village. Buffalo meat is hung to dry in background. From a painting (1834) in Catlin's Indian Gallery. *Courtesy, Smithsonian Institution.*

Indians hunting buffalo by stampeding them over a cliff. From a watercolor by Miller. *Courtesy, Walters Art Gallery.*

ing them over cliffs, by driving them into canyons where they could be shot at leisure, and by shooting them with bows and arrows (and later with guns) from horseback. The greatest delicacies were the buffalo hump, the tongue, and the intestines (which Indians particularly relished and which many mountain men regarded as dainty food).

The coming of the railroads spelled the end of the buffalo. White hunters and sportsmen, many from Europe, swarmed to the buffalo country and slaughtered the stupid beasts in untold numbers. Thousands were killed merely for their hides, though buffalo meat was shipped back East and sold in the markets. Other thousands were shot merely in what passed for "sport." Even Francis Parkman in *The Oregon Trail* devoted a whole chapter to the joys of the wholesale slaughter of buffalo. If the sportsman took any portion of the buffalo to camp for food, he usually contented himself with the tongue or a piece of the hump.

English noblemen and German princelings heard about the sport of buffalo hunting and came in droves to take part in the slaughter. But most of the buffalo were killed by

A buffalo hunt with bow and arrow. From a painting (1830's) in Catlin's Indian Galley. *Courtesy, Walters Art Gallery.*

A Texas longhorn roped by a cowboy. From a photograph by F. M. Steele, in the collections of the Library of Congress.

hired hunters who for years supplied the hide markets of the East. Buffalo robes were prized as lap robes for buggies and sleighs, and leather made from buffalo hides was an important article of commerce.

By 1875 the buffalo were so diminished that the survivors were found in only two herds, one south of the Union Pacific Railroad and the other to the north. Within three years most of the southern herd had been exterminated, and by 1884 the northern herd was virtually gone. Two years later an official of the Smithsonian Institution pointed out that the American buffalo (or bison) would soon be extinct unless something was done about it, and a campaign began that rescued the buffalo from complete extinction. No longer could the Indians depend on the buffalo for sustenance. Penned on their reservations, the Indians had to subsist on such cattle as they could raise or beg from the government.

As the buffalo disappeared, ranchers moved into the grazing country with herds of cattle, which quickly multiplied and established an industry—and an element of romance—that left a deep impress on American life. Many people think of the frontier almost exclusively in terms of the cattle country and cowboys.

Long before the forty-niners started for California, cattle that the Spaniards had brought to America had filled the plains of Mexico, parts of Texas, and southern California. By the time Texas had become a state of the Union, Texas cattle were already important in the life of the West. These cattle were a mixed breed, unlike any other American cattle. J. Frank Dobie, in a fascinating book called *The Longhorns*, has given a full account of the varieties of Texas cattle, the most distinctive being the longhorns, which developed from the original Moorish cattle of the Spaniards, mixed with other breeds that settlers on the edge of the frontier brought with them. These rangy, tough beasts with huge, spreading horns were the characteristic Texas cattle before the development of modern beef types. They grazed the unfenced Texas plains, guarded by cow-

Vaqueros demonstrate their skill in roping cattle. From a photograph of a watercolor, in the collections of the Library of Congress.

A cattle chute on the Kansas Pacific Railway at Abilene. From *Leslie's Illustrated* (1871). Courtesy, Library of Congress.

boys who had learned their craft from Mexican *vaqueros*. Early travelers in Mexico and California were astonished at the *vaqueros'* skill in roping cattle with their rawhide *reatas*. American cattlemen acquired the art of swinging a lariat from a galloping horse, roping cattle by horns or heels, throwing, and branding them with a particular mark designating their ownership.

In the 1850's, 1860's, and 1870's millions of acres of grass yet unclaimed and unfenced by farmers offered a range for cattle. After the passage of the Homestead Act, ranchers frequently took up a homestead of 160 acres on a watercourse and turned their cattle out to range the free government lands surrounding their homestead. An unwritten understanding among cattlemen prevented ranchers from encroaching on the grazing territory already occupied by another's cattle. As yet farmers were not moving in to claim land on the open ranges. That time would come later, with conflict between cattlemen and nesters, as ranchers called the homesteading farmers.

Before the Civil War, Texas produced more cattle than the ranchers could market. But the scarcity of cattle after the war and the coming of the railroads increased the demand in the East. Then began the long drives of Texas cattle to railheads in Kansas and the growth of Kansas cow towns like Abilene and Dodge City. Once the cattle reached a railway center, buyers were on hand to purchase and ship the animals to market in St. Louis and other points East.

Much of the folklore of the cowboy originated in the long cattle drives from Texas to Kansas. A farsighted promoter named Joseph G. McCoy, from Illinois, conceived the notion of establishing a shipping center at Abilene in 1867, for Abilene was conveniently located on the Kansas Pacific Railway and McCoy believed that Texas cattle could reach Abilene without crossing settled farming lands. He later wrote an account of his enterprise, *Historic Sketches of the Cattle Trade of the West and Southwest* (1874), which provided firsthand descriptions of the industry. Dodge City developed as another shipping center soon after Abilene.

The price difference of cattle in Texas and Kansas made the long drive feasible. A steer that was worth $8 to $10 in Texas would bring $28 after reaching Abilene and fattening for a month on Kansas grass. Consequently, after 1867, an ever-increasing number of Texas cattle started north each spring.

Driving herds of hundreds of steers was a tricky business, requiring experienced cowhands willing to endure hardships and face innumerable hazards of the trail. Cows are temperamental creatures, and Texas longhorns were among the most unpredictable of beasts. The greatest danger of the drive was in stampedes, wild and frenzied panics that sent the whole herd thundering off in any direction, sometimes over cliffs to their destruction. Consequently the herders had to be constantly on the alert to prevent, if possible, the start of a stampede.

Cowboys and chuck wagons at a roundup. From a photograph by Grabill, in the collections of the Library of Congress.

The organization of the team responsible for the drive took care and forethought. First, an experienced trail boss had to be selected. He then picked out eight to ten men whom he could trust in any emergency. And last, but not least, he recruited the best cook he could find. The cook was in charge of the chuck wagon, a wonderfully well-organized vehicle with a compartmented box standing at the rear for flour, meal, sugar, salt, bacon, molasses, and other foodstuffs. The back of this box would let down to form a worktable for the cook when he stopped to prepare a meal. The wagon also carried a barrel of water and perhaps a keg of rum for "emergencies." In the front of the wagon, the cowboys stowed blankets, tarpaulins, extra lariats, and a supply of rawhide strips, needed for mending everything from a broken bridle to a split wagon tongue.

The usual herd consisted of about 2,500 steers, though the number might vary within limits of a few hundred more or less. The larger the herd, the greater the danger of stampedes. On the first day of the drive the cowboys drove the herd hard, perhaps making 25 miles before allowing them to bed down for the night. The theory was that a tired herd would be less liable to stampede. After a few days of travel, the pace slowed down. The herd was allowed to graze in the early morning, while the men ate a breakfast of flapjacks, bacon, maybe young beef, and molasses. The cattle were then driven until noon, when, with good luck, they reached a water hole or stream. They were allowed to rest, while the men had a midday snack. The afternoon drive usually tried to reach a stream and good pasturage, though sometimes cattle and men had to make a dry camp.

After the cattle bedded down, cowboys on duty had the responsibility of keeping them quiet and undisturbed. One way to calm them was to ride slowly around the herd singing to them. Cowboys firmly believed that singing to the beasts would keep them from taking fright. But sometimes no songs could prevent a panic. A summer storm with thunder and lightning might send the brutes plunging into the dark. The howling of a coyote, even the sudden breaking of a stick, or any unusual noise could wake up a restless steer, and one snort might start the whole herd. At such times the night men rode around the herd, trying to send the cattle racing in a circle. Then they would wind themselves into a pack and finally stop from sheer impact

Cowboys slowly circling the herd after a long day's drive. From a wood engraving after Frenzeny & Tavernier, in *Harper's Weekly* (March 28, 1874).

Cowboys roaring into town for Christmas. From an engraving after a drawing by Remington, in *Harper's Weekly* (October 13, 1877).

on one another. So great was the panic on occasion, however, that cattle in the inner circle would be crushed to death. A herd of 2,500 maddened longhorns, clashing together, was a fearsome sight. Sometimes they ran over both the cowboy and his horse, and more than one luckless cattleman thus met his death on the "lone prairie."

Other hazards might be encountered on the long trail to Kansas. Part of the route led through territory still occupied by Indians who were not averse to stampeding the herds and picking off strays for their own use. Even when friendly, the Indians sometimes exacted a fee of 10 cents or more for each head of cattle that crossed their land. As Kansas began to develop a cattle industry of its own, efforts were made to restrict entry of Texas cattle, because they brought ticks that caused the dreaded tick fever. Increasing problems and costs, plus the growing hostility of Kansas and Nebraska to Texas cattle being driven into their territories, gradually brought the long drive to an end.

Finally, the railroads pushed lines into Texas which made the overland trek unnecessary.

The long drive left a rich heritage of American folklore. Fiction, movies, and television still make capital of rip-roaring days in Abilene, Dodge City, Newton, Ellsworth, and other cow towns, where every other building housed a saloon or gambling resort; the towns were wide open when the cowboys delivered their herds and were ready to let off steam. Cardsharps, loose women, and every type of shyster flocked to these frontier towns to separate the cattle drovers from their money. Gunplay was common, and the cemeteries of some towns grew almost as fast as the permanent population. Recollections of these events have provided both local historians and fiction writers with a rich vein of ore, which they continue to mine.

The demand for beef in the East made cattle ranching in Kansas, Nebraska, and elsewhere in the West profitable and saw the proliferation of the cowboy and his way of life. But gradually immigrant farmers, eager for free land under the Homestead Act, began to filter into the range country in constantly increasing numbers. Inevitably this brought the farmer into conflict with the cattleman. As 160-acre farms multiplied, the old free range, where cattle could graze at will on government land, continued to dwindle. At first the cattlemen waged a ruthless war on the farmers. Many a farmer was driven from his homestead at the point of a gun or frightened away by threats against the safety of his wife and children. But slowly farmers gained on the cattle ranchers, who were forced to retreat to regions not yet taken over by farms.

Cattlemen faced another invasion in the high plains from sheepherders. Sheep, the cattlemen claimed, nipped the grass so close that they ruined pasturage for cattle. So the cattlemen made an effort to drive out the sheepherders. In some areas they drove thousands of sheep over cliffs; elsewhere they simply murdered the herders. But the price of wool was high, and sheep proved more profitable than cattle.

223

A sheep raid in Colorado. From a wood engraving after Frenzeny, in *Harper's Weekly* (October 13, 1877).

In some instances, cattlemen themselves saw the light and switched to sheep. At any rate sheep raising got a foothold in the West which it has maintained to the present day.

An invention in 1874 helped transform the cattle industry and bring about a revolution that permitted ranching and farming in the same area. In that year a farmer named Joseph F. Glidden, of De Kalb, Illinois, conceived the notion of making a wire fence with twisted barbs at intervals along the strands of wire. He had invented barbed wire. Unlike many inventors, he patented his device and lived to reap a profit from the manufacture of barbed wire, which quickly found eager purchasers. Within the next two decades, barbed wire was being used to fence in pasturage and to keep cattle within bounds. Now farmers and ranchers could inhabit the same county in peace.

A mass movement of farmers that exceeded the earlier migrations of miners began about 1870 and continued for the next thirty years. Thousands of farmers along the old Mississippi frontier pulled up stakes and moved farther West in search of fresh land that they could take up free. Others bought cheap land. From the older settled regions of the East farmers also flocked to the Great Plains. Emigration from Europe, stimulated by the advertisements of steamship companies which told of the prosperity to be found in America, showed a continuous increase during the last three decades of the nineteenth century. Many emigrants from Ireland, Germany, Norway, Denmark, and Sweden settled in the West. The bitter winters of Minnesota and the Dakotas did not discourage the Scandinavians, who made up a substantial portion of the new population in those regions. Nor did the blizzards which swept Nebraska and western Kansas turn back settlers who had learned that fat harvests of wheat could be expected from the black soil of the prairies.

Life was not easy for these pioneers, but they persisted in coming in ever swelling numbers; they gradually filled up the vacant land of the Great Plains, built crude houses,

A group of Swedish emigrants headed West. From a wood engraving in *Gleason's Pictorial* (October 30, 1852).

A sod house in Nebraska. From a photograph by S. D. Butcher (c. 1877), in the collections of the Library of Congress.

established towns, and began to lay the foundations of a civilized way of life.

The first dwellings of settlers in many portions of Nebraska, western Kansas, and other areas lacking in timber were dugouts and sod houses. If a hillside could be found, it was easy to hollow out a cavern and wall it up with blocks of sod. The prairie grass sufficed to hold the squares of earth together so that they could be used like adobe brick farther West.

The flat prairie, however, usually offered no hillside to provide a place for a cavern. Then the whole house had to be made of blocks of turf. Usually enough cottonwood poles could be found along some stream to provide a frame for a roof, made of thatched grass, covered with light turf to hold the thatch in place against the winter winds. If a few boards could be found, a door would be made, but often a cowhide had to serve.

A mud and stick chimney made a flue for a fireplace of stones or homemade bricks. The floor, of course, was of packed earth, sometimes covered with a buffalo robe, a cowhide, or a bearskin. Furniture was homemade: rawhide strips stretched across a wooden frame with straw-filled ticks for a bed; a few crude benches; deer's antlers fastened to the wall for a clothes rack; a rough wooden table; a few pots, an iron skillet, a Dutch oven; and that about accounted for household furnishings. All cooking, of course, was done over the open fire.

Such crude houses, of course, were endured only until the pioneers could establish themselves, earn enough from their crops to buy lumber delivered at the nearest railway station, and erect frame houses. In a surprisingly short time, more comfortable houses began to dot the prairies. The frontiersmen of the late nineteenth century did not endure hardship from choice, as the mountain men had done. They were eager to reestablish as quickly as possible the civilized way of life they had earlier known.

Schoolhouses and churches were among the first permanent structures built. Not only did they serve the usual purposes of education and religion, but they also provided the

A sod schoolhouse in Kansas. From a photograph by J. H. Young (1907), in the collections of the Library of Congress.

The power of music—itinerant fiddlers provided most of the music known on the frontier. From a lithograph by A. & C. Kaufman after a painting by A. Dircks (1872). *Courtesy, Library of Congress.*

whole community, old and young, with centers for a variety of social activities. In fact, about the only opportunities for social contacts of the community as a whole came at the schools and at the churches.

The schoolhouse was often only a one-room affair with one teacher who was expected to give instruction in everything from the ABC's to Latin. Nevertheless, it served as a gathering place where young people met on Saturday nights to practice home talent plays or to hold song recitals. The only musical instrument, except a mouth organ, that was common in early frontier communities was the fiddle, and many of the stricter sects regarded it as the devil's instrument. But if the community was not dominated by the more puritanical sects, a fiddler might be engaged for square dances at the schoolhouse. Occasionally several fiddlers gathered at what was announced as a fiddlers' convention, and everybody sprightly enough to dance took part in a regular hoedown. If, however, Methodists, Baptists, Dutch Reformed, or any of the other stricter Protestant sects were too numerous, fiddling and dancing could not contaminate the schoolhouse.

Nobody objected to the use of the schoolhouse for debates, for recitations by traveling "elocution" teachers and local lovers of the limelight, or for oratorical contests. Many a prairie politician got his first taste for public speaking in the neighborhood school. Friday afternoon was usually given over to the recital of speeches, many of them learned from *McGuffey's Fifth* or *Sixth Reader*. "Spartacus to the Gladiators" was a favorite, as was Marc Antony's funeral oration over Caesar.

Spelling bees were also favorite forms of extracurricular entertainment. Matches were arranged between pupils of various ages, between boys and girls, between women and men, and between champion spellers from other communities. The blue-back spelling book was the authority that determined correctness of spelling and pronunciation. Prizes were given for the best spellers and the matches created as much excitement as a horse race.

The churches, whatever their religious persuasion, were less given to worldly entertainment, but pioneer congregations got a great deal of satisfaction out of sermons that sometimes ran on for more than an hour. Even those citi-

The church dominates an 1866 view of the mining town of Black Hawk, Colorado. From a lithograph by J. Bien after a sketch in Mathews, *Pencil Sketches.*

zens who did not profess great piety sometimes became connoisseurs of sermons and went to church for the intellectual exercise of appraising the parson's utterances. For some curious reason, blacksmiths and medical doctors frequently were numbered among the unbelievers and delighted in shocking the orthodox by expressing heretical views.

The churches were more important as social institutions on the frontier than in urban areas today, for they served as instruments of social cohesion that often kept neighborhoods from falling apart. They provided weekly meeting places where neighbors met to exchange news, keep in touch with each other, and arrange for mutual help when and where it was needed. Before and after the regular service, churchgoers stood about in the yard and talked, sometimes for an hour or more. Occasionally, during revival services, called big meetings, members brought picnic dinners of enticing magnitude, listened to a sermon in the morning, ate an enormous meal at midday, and heard another sermon in the afternoon if they could keep awake.

Sundays were also occasions when young people could meet for a bit of surreptitious courting under pretense of practicing for the choir or getting ready for some extra service at Christmas or Easter. Whatever the denomination, churches were highly useful in helping people, scattered over distant farms, in maintaining contacts.

Leisure in frontier communities was virtually nonexistent, and opportunities when young and old could gather at the schoolhouse or the church were highly prized. Our present age, which is concerned with developing ways to utilize surplus leisure, has little realization of how little spare time our ancestors had. Not even those in older, settled communities were burdened with leisure; people developing new lands had even less.

Women especially found their work endless. Not only did they have the normal duties that fall to females—the bearing and nurture of children—but they had the making of clothing for the whole family, for the men and boys, as well as for the women and girls. They had the preparation of three meals each day, meals for a growing and hungry family with enormous appetites. No laborsaving devices were available. As children got old enough, they could be put to shelling peas, peeling potatoes, and wielding a churn dasher, but many a housewife had no children old enough to help.

She also had the washing to do, with soap that she made from fat carefully saved and boiled with lye caught from the leachings of wood ashes. Water was often scarce and had to be brought from a distant stream or spring. Women had no time for frivolity. How they managed to get through their daily duties baffles the imagination. Yet there are few records of complaints, grievances, frustrations, or divorces. People, male or female, had little time to feel sorry for themselves, and nobody had yet learned that "frustrations" were something to condemn one to unhappiness.

The pioneer farmer characteristically ate well. The first thing he thought about after making a habitable house was to lay out a garden and plant vegetable seeds. He set out

Saturday afternoon chore—helping Grandmother. From a Currier & Ives lithograph (c. 1865). *Courtesy, Library of Congress.*

an orchard as soon as he could procure a stock of fruit trees. He usually brought with him poultry (chickens, turkeys, ducks, and geese), and he tried to fix a pen for them that would keep out coyotes. A pigpen far enough from his house so that it would not offend his nostrils, but not so far that marauding bears would steal his pigs, gave promise of pork. A cow or two provided milk and butter. Curiously, in the cow country, ranchers had less milk and butter than other people. They kept few cows for milk. Occasionally, when ill-health required milk for an invalid, a rancher would have a cow with a young calf lassoed and milked for enough to sustain the patient.

Pioneer gardens grew the usual vegetables: beans, peas, squash, pumpkins, turnips, cabbage, potatoes (both white and sweet), beets, and anything else the owner's fancy might dictate or the soil might produce. Unlike modern housewives who can depend on canned or frozen foods, the frontier women had to spend time drying vegetables for winter use. Squash and pumpkins were cut into long slices and hung up to dry. Fresh corn was also cut from the cob and dried. Indeed, Indian corn was a food of many uses. Fresh roasting ears were eaten all summer; the dried green corn could be soaked and made into fresh-tasting dishes in winter; the mature corn could be ground into grits, which took the place of rice, or ground finer into meal, which made bread or mush, or soaked in lye and washed clear of the husks and eaten as big hominy. Few of the raw materials of food could be served in more ways than corn.

In the spring the prairie itself provided edibles. Dandelions were gathered for salad greens, as were several other weeds, such as pokeberry and lamb's-quarters. Housewives also searched the fields for herbs which they believed had medicinal values. Some they beat up and made into poultices for swellings and wounds; others they boiled for tea and drank to "purify the blood."

The staple of frontier diet, of course, was meat. Fresh

Frontiersmen returning from the hunt with wild game for the larder. From a Currier & Ives lithograph (1867). *Courtesy, Library of Congress.*

pork was eaten in cold weather, but enough was salted and cured as bacon, hams, and shoulders to last during the summer. Beef was eaten less frequently than pork. Occasionally a young yearling was slaughtered for fresh meat; any surplus that could not be eaten at once was dried or pickled. Steak was normally pounded, peppered, salted, floured, and fried. Steaks broiled rare, which we today regard as the best form of beef, were not common on frontier tables. Farm families ate an astonishing amount of boiled meats of various kinds, frequently made into stews with vegetables, fresh or dried. When the men on the farm had time to hunt, the larder was replenished with wild game: venison, bear, coon, possum, wild duck, and partridge. A legend reports that Missouri pioneers were so fond of possum that they carried a few along when they went to California, and escaping possum established the breed on the West Coast.

A flourishing farm in the West, 1871. From a Currier & Ives lithograph (1871) in the collections of the Library of Congress.

Water was often a problem for the early pioneers on the Great Plains. When possible, they settled on a watercourse. But they often found themselves in regions where they could not find well water at normal depths. Deep well drilling was costly, but gradually, as prosperity increased, windmills pumping water from deep wells dotted the landscape. It was the usual practice for farmers to make dams across ditches and ravines to catch water for their livestock during the winter rains and snows. This water, they hoped, would last through the dry months.

In time, in fact in a remarkably short time, the Western frontiersmen of the last three decades of the nineteenth century subdued a difficult terrain and made the land bring forth bountiful crops of wheat, corn, and other grains. They improved their livestock and enriched their farms They built better houses and added luxuries. In short, be· fore the end of the century, the farmers of the West for the most part were flourishing, towns were growing, and the era when the land was described as the Great American Desert was forgotten.

But nature was not altogether kind. A series of good years made the inhabitants of some of the drier parts of the West believe that the country would always have enough rainfall. A few scientists even argued that planting the land had changed the climate. Wet years, however, were followed by drought after drought, and some farmers were ruined. They had to learn new techniques of dry farming—cultivation that harrows the soil to keep it pulverized after every rainfall to prevent evaporation. In time dry farming or irrigation made even the dry lands again prosperous.

The frontiersman in the West did his best to reproduce the best of the civilization he had previously known. When he had subdued the land, he set about building schools and colleges. In few areas has the population paid so much attention to education as in the West. Where buffalo and Indians roamed less than a century ago, now one may find the campuses of some of the great universities of the country. These did not merely happen. They are a symbol of the hard work, the aspirations, and the dreams of a vigorous and determined people anxious to create a civilization in which they could take pride.

Horace Greeley Finds Some Homesteaders Shiftless (1859)

Horace Greeley, the New York newspaper editor who coined the phrase "Go West, young man," made a trip through the West in 1859. He wrote an account of his experiences, which he published in 1850 with the title *An Overland Journey*. Not all homesteaders, he discovered, were sturdy, thrifty citizens. In the passage below he comments on some settlers he encountered in Kansas.

I met at Osawatamie an old Whig and now Republican friend who left New York City (where he had been an industrious mechanic) and settled between Lawrence and

Westward the course of empire takes its way. From a Currier & Ives lithograph after F. F. Palmer. *Courtesy, Library of Congress.*

Topeka two years ago. He had last year eighty acres in corn, which yielded four thousand bushels, worth to him thirty-five or forty cents per bushel. His clear profit on this corn, above the immediate cost of growing it, can hardly have been less than one thousand dollars. He will grow more this year, with wheat, potatoes, etc.; yet he is one of a class who are popularly supposed incapable of making money by farming. I suspect few lifelong farmers of simi- lar means will have good buildings over their heads and fruit trees and other elements of material comfort around them sooner than my friend.

Wheat and oats did badly last year, owing to the heavy summer rains which rusted and blighted them. Too little of either have been sown for this year's harvest, yet I find both winter and spring wheat looking remarkably well al- most everywhere. Oats are scarcely more than out of the ground; yet they, too, promise well, so far as can now be foreseen.

But an unpleasant truth must be stated: There are too many idle, shiftless people in Kansas. I speak not here of lawyers, gentlemen speculators, and other nonproducers, who are in excess here as elsewhere; I allude directly to those who call themselves settlers, and who would be farm- ers if they were anything. To see a man squatted on a quarter section in a cabin which would make a fair hogpen, but is unfit for a human habitation, and there living from

Where buffalo and Indians had roamed, students soon flocked to the campuses of great universities. The University of Wisconsin at Madison in 1879. From a lithograph by Beck & Pauli (1879). *Courtesy, Library of Congress.*

hand to mouth by a little of this and a little of that, with hardly an acre of prairie broken (sometimes without a fence up), with no garden, no fruit trees, "no nothing"— waiting for someone to come along and buy out his "claim" and let him move on to repeat the operation somewhere else—this is enough to give a cheerful man the horrors. Ask the squatter what he means, and he can give you a hundred good excuses for his miserable condition: he has no breaking team; he has little or no good rail timber; he has had the "shakes"; his family have been sick; he lost two years and some stock by the border ruffians, etc., etc. But all this don't overbear the facts that, if *he* has no good timber, some of his neighbors have it in abundance, and would be very glad to have him work part of it into rails on shares at a fair rate; and if he has no breaking team, he can hire out in haying and harvest, and get nearly or quite two acres broken next month for every faithful week's work he chooses to give at that busy season. The poorest man ought thus to be able to get ten acres broken, fenced, and into crop, each year. For poor men gradually hew farms out of heavy timber, where every fenced and cultivated acre has cost twice to thrice the work it does here.

237

And it is sad to note that hardly half the settlers make any sort of provision for wintering their cattle, even by cutting a stack of prairie hay, when every good day's work will put up a ton of it. If he has a cornfield, the squatter's cattle are welcome to pick at that all winter; if he has none, they must go into the bottoms and browse through as best they can. Hence his calves are miserable affairs; his cows unfit to make butter from till the best of the season is over; his oxen, should he have a pair, must be recruiting from their winter's famine just when he most urgently needs their work. And this exposing cattle all winter to these fierce prairie winds, is alike inhuman and wasteful. I asked a settler the other day how he *could* do it? "I had no time to make a shelter for them." "But had you no Sundays?—did you not have these at your disposal?" "O, yes? I don't work Sundays." "Well, you *should* have worked every one of them, rather than let your cattle shiver in the cold blasts all winter—it would have been a work of humanity and mercy to cut and haul logs, get up a cattle stall, and cover it with prairie hay, which I will warrant to be more religious than anything you did on those Sundays." But the squatter was of a different opinion.

How a man located in a little squalid cabin on one of these rich "claims" can sleep moonlit nights under the average circumstances of his class passes my comprehension. I should want to work moderately but resolutely, at least fourteen hours of each secular day, until I had made myself comfortable, with a fence around at least eighty acres, a quarter of this partitioned off for my working cattle, a decent, warm shelter to cover them in cold or stormy weather, a tolerable habitation for my family, at least forty acres in crop, and a young orchard growing. For one commencing with next to nothing, I estimate this as the work of five years; after which, he might take things more easily, awaiting the fruit from his orchard and the coming up of his boys to help him. But for the first four or five years, the poor pioneer should work every hour that he does not absolutely need for rest. Every hour's work then will save him many hours in after life.

For the farmer who comes in with liberal means, the

task is obviously much easier. Let us suppose one to be worth $5,000 the day he lands on the Kansas shore of the Missouri, and see how quickly he can make a farm and a home. He arrives, we will say, in August, when he can see just what the country produces, whether in a state of nature or under cultivation. He buys a quarter section (which is land enough for any man) in a choice locality, including thirty or forty acres of timbered river or creek bottom, say for $10 per acre, charges $1,000 of the $1,600 thus called for to the account of the proslavery democracy, for defeating the free land bill, and sets to work, with two good hired men. He buys five yoke of oxen for a breaking team, a span of good wagon horses, a cow in fresh milk, and three heifers which will be cows next spring, puts up a cabin that will just do, and is ready to commence breaking by the 1st of September. As his men break, he follows with the horses, sowing and harrowing in wheat so long as that will answer, but does not stop breaking till the ground is frozen. Now he begins to cut and draw timber for a fitter habitation to which to welcome his family in the spring. Having done this, he gets good mechanics to finish it, while he and his men go to work at fencing, by cutting saw logs for light, narrow boards, if there be a sawmill convenient; if not, then by cutting for and splitting rails. So soon as the driest land will answer for it, he begins to put in spring wheat, then oats, then corn, putting up fence whenever the soil is too wet for plowing. Let him not forget to have a few acres seasonably set in fruit trees, some of them dwarfs for early bearing. Thus his money will not have been exhausted by the ensuing fall, when he will have crops coming in and more than a hundred acres of his land broken and subdued for future cultivation. I see no reason why a resolute, good manager should not be comfortable after his first year or two, and henceforth take the world as easily as need be.

Teddy Roosevelt Writes
About Cowboys (1885-88)

Theodore Roosevelt, twenty-sixth President of the United States, known as Teddy Roosevelt, spent three years as a young man on a ranch in what was then the Dakota Territory. He told of his experiences in a volume, *Ranch Life and the Hunting-Trail,* first published in 1888, a fascinating book about the West. In the passage below he talks about cow towns and cowboys.

A true "cow town" is worth seeing—such a one as Miles City, for instance, especially at the time of the annual meeting of the great Montana Stock Raisers' Association. Then the whole place is full to overflowing, the importance of the meeting and the fun of the attendant frolics, especially the horse races, drawing from the surrounding ranch country many hundreds of men of every degree, from the rich stockowner worth his millions to the ordinary cowboy who works for forty dollars a month. It would be impossible to imagine a more typically American assemblage, for although there are always a certain number of foreigners, usually English, Irish, or German, yet they have become completely Americanized; and on the whole it would be difficult to gather a finer body of men, in spite of their numerous shortcomings. The ranch owners differ more from each other than do the cowboys; and the former certainly compare very favorably with similar classes of capitalists in the East. Anything more foolish than the demagogic outcry against "cattle kings" it would be difficult to imagine. Indeed, there are very few businesses so absolutely legitimate as stock raising and so beneficial to the nation at large; and a successful stock grower must not only be shrewd, thrifty, patient, and enterprising, but he must also possess qualities of personal bravery, hardihood, and self-reliance to a degree not demanded in the least by any mercantile occupation in a community long settled. Stockmen are in the West the pioneers of civilization, and their daring and adventurousness make the after settlement of the region possible. The whole country owes them a great debt.

The most successful ranchmen are those, usually Southwesterners, who have been bred to the business and have grown up with it; but many Eastern men, including not a few college graduates, have also done excellently by devot-

240

ing their whole time and energy to their work—although Easterners who invest their money in cattle without knowing anything of the business, or who trust all to their subordinates, are naturally enough likely to incur heavy losses. Stockmen are learning more and more to act together; and certainly the meetings of their associations are conducted with a dignity and good sense that would do credit to any parliamentary body.

But the cowboys resemble one another much more and outsiders much less than is the case even with their employers, the ranchmen. A town in the cattle country, when for some cause it is thronged with men from the neighborhood, always presents a picturesque sight. On the wooden sidewalks of the broad, dusty streets the men who ply the various industries known only to frontier existence jostle one another as they saunter to and fro or lounge lazily in front of the straggling, cheap-looking board houses. Hunters come in from the plains and the mountains, clad in buckskin shirts and fur caps, greasy and unkempt, but with resolute faces and sullen, watchful eyes, that are ever on the alert. The teamsters, surly and self-contained, wear slouch hats and great cowhide boots; while the stage drivers, their faces seamed by the hardship and exposure of their long drives with every kind of team, through every kind of country, and in every kind of weather, proud of their really wonderful skill as reinsmen and conscious of their high standing in any frontier community, look down on and sneer at the "skin hunters" and the plodding drivers of the white-topped prairie schooners.

Besides these there are trappers, and wolfers, whose business is to poison wolves, with shaggy, knock-kneed ponies to carry their small bales and bundles of furs—beaver, wolf, fox, and occasionally otter; and silent sheepherders, with cast-down faces, never able to forget the absolute solitude and monotony of their dreary lives, nor to rid their minds of the thought of the woolly idiots they pass all their days in tending.

Such are the men who have come to town, either on business or else to frequent the flaunting saloons and gaudy hells of all kinds in search of the coarse, vicious excitement that in the minds of many of them does duty as pleasure—the only form of pleasure they have ever had a chance to know. Indians too, wrapped in blankets, with stolid, emotionless faces, stalk silently 'round among the whites, or join in the gambling and horse racing.

If the town is on the borders of the mountain country, there will also be sinewy lumbermen, rough-looking miners, and packers, whose business it is to guide the long mule and pony trains that go where wagons cannot and whose work in packing needs special and peculiar skill; and mingled with and drawn from all these classes are desperadoes of every grade, from the gambler up through the horse thief to the murderous professional bully, or, as he is locally called, "bad man"—now, however, a much less conspicuous object than formerly.

But everywhere among these plainsmen and mountain men, and more important than any, are the cowboys—the men who follow the calling that has brought such towns into being. Singly, or in twos or threes, they gallop their wiry little horses down the street, their lithe, supple figures erect or swaying slightly as they sit loosely in the saddle; while their stirrups are so long that their knees are hardly bent, the bridles not taut enough to keep the chains from clanking. They are smaller and less muscular than the wielders of ax and pick; but they are as hardy and self-reliant as any men who ever breathed—with bronzed, set faces, and keen eyes that look all the world straight in the face without flinching as they flash out from under the broad-brimmed hats. Peril and hardship, and years of long toil broken by weeks of brutal dissipation, draw haggard lines across their eager faces, but never dim their reckless eyes nor break their bearing of defiant self-confidence. They do not walk well, partly because they so rarely do any work out of the saddle, partly because their *chaperaios* or leather overalls hamper them when on the ground; but their appearance is striking for all that, and picturesque too, with their jingling spurs, the big revolvers stuck in their belts, and bright silk handkerchiefs knotted loosely round their necks over the open collars of the flannel shirts.

When drunk on the villainous whisky of the frontier

242

towns, they cut mad antics, riding their horses into the saloons, firing their pistols right and left, from boisterous lightheartedness rather than from any viciousness, and indulging too often in deadly shooting affrays, brought on either by the accidental contact of the moment or on account of some long-standing grudge, or perhaps because of bad blood between two ranches or localities; but except while on such sprees they are quiet, rather self-contained men, perfectly frank and simple, and on their own ground treat a stranger with the most whole-souled hospitality, doing all in their power for him and scorning to take any reward in return. Although prompt to resent an injury, they are not at all apt to be rude to outsiders, treating them with what can almost be called a grave courtesy. They are much better fellows and pleasanter companions than small farmers or agricultural laborers; nor are the mechanics and workmen of a great city to be mentioned in the same breath.

The bulk of the cowboys themselves are Southwesterners; but there are also many from the Eastern and the Northern states, who, if they begin young, do quite as well as the Southerners. The best hands are fairly bred to the work and follow it from their youth up. Nothing can be more foolish than for an Easterner to think he can become a cowboy in a few months' time. Many a young fellow comes out hot with enthusiasm for life on the plains, only to learn that his clumsiness is greater than he could have believed possible; that the cowboy business is like any other and has to be learned by serving a painful apprenticeship; and that this apprenticeship implies the endurance of rough fare, hard living, dirt, exposure of every kind, no little toil, and month after month of the dullest monotony.

For cowboy work there is need of special traits and special training, and young Easterners should be sure of themselves before trying it: the struggle for existence is very keen in the Far West, and it is no place for men who lack the ruder, coarser virtues and physical qualities, no matter how intellectual or how refined and delicate their sensibilities. Such are more likely to fail there than in older communities.

Cowboys, like most Westerners, occasionally show remarkable versatility in their tastes and pursuits. One whom I know has abandoned his regular occupation for the past nine months, during which time he has been in succession a bartender, a schoolteacher, and a probate judge! Another, whom I once employed for a short while, had passed through even more varied experiences, including those of a barber, a sailor, an apothecary, and a buffalo hunter.

As a rule the cowboys are known to each other only by their first names, with, perhaps, as a prefix, the title of the brand for which they are working. Thus I remember once overhearing a casual remark to the effect that "Bar Y Harry" had married "the Seven Open A girl," the latter being the daughter of a neighboring ranchman. Often they receive nicknames, as, for instance, Dutch Wannigan, Windy Jack, and Kid Williams, all of whom are on the list of my personal acquaintances.

Epilogue: A People in Motion

In the filling up of the North American continent, many influences have been at work. From the beginning, land speculators busied themselves. During the opening of the first frontiers east of the Mississippi, land companies played an important part. Greed for gold and other minerals sent an avalanche of migrants to the distant shores of the Pacific. Later speculators, sellers of mine stocks, and purveyors of land titles lured immigrants westward. The railroads, with great acreages of land obtained free from the government, also in time became real estate promoters. The Homestead Act added the incentive of free land for anyone with the tenacity to develop 160 acres of prairie or desert. From the days of Jamestown to our own time, the West has had attractions of many kinds to draw people to it. More recently the West may have offered no better lure than the tawdry tinsel of Hollywood, but nevertheless, it continues to attract. A frontier of sorts still exists in the imaginations of many people. For some mystical reason the magnetic pull has been prevailingly westward since the beginning of our history.

A land-office business—in a Kansas land office. From a wood engraving after Frenzeny & Tavernier, in *Harper's Weekly* (July 11, 1874).

In earlier days the acquisition of land exerted a powerful incentive. Our generation has seen a reversal of the migration to the country. Few men now turn to the land, except a scattering who want to be gentlemen farmers and others who think a farm will lose enough money to reduce their income tax burden. The attraction of our generation has been to the cities which have grown into vast metropolitan areas. But in city growth the West has continued its fascination for migrants. Los Angeles, for example, sprawls over miles of barren hills and valleys, filled with people recently arrived. As a nation, we are restless, continually searching for something we do not find. Many of our people in past generations established farms in Missouri, grew dissatisfied and moved on into Iowa. After a time among the green fields of Iowa, Nebraska and Kansas beckoned, and they left for more distant prairie lands. Their sons often sold out and crossed the mountains into California to become ranchers, orchardists, chicken farmers, oil magnates, airplane manufacturers, or bankers. Always we have been in motion, and we continue to move about, from country to town, from city to city, ever in search of El Dorado, happiness, contentment, something.

Several years ago, Professor George W. Pierson of Yale published a thoughtful essay in the *Yale Review* (1954) entitled "The Moving American." "There is a fever in our blood," he declared. "We have itching feet. Here today and gone tomorrow. Let's go. 'Scuse our dust. Fill 'er up. Free wheeling. Howdy, stranger. As early as 1831 Alexis de Tocqueville was stunned by the sheer restlessness of Jacksonian America. After moving to America, the German Francis Lieber declared he felt all the time as if tied to the wing of a windmill. . . . The automobile 'restated the national principle'—and today there isn't anything Americans won't do on wheels: eat, drink, sleep, or propagate the race. The Americans, says a horrified Frenchman, even 'make love in the automobile.' Also [make] a bank deposit. For we have drive-in banks, drive-in restaurants, drive-in theaters, and drive-in churches. . . ."

The frenzy for movement, for going ever toward some distant goal, is even greater today than it was during the height of the westward movement, Mr. Pierson declared. For at the time 20 percent of the population lived in regions where they were not born, whereas today nearly 24 percent of the population lives outside its native states.

Our restlessness has been prompted in a large measure by our optimism. We constantly hope to better ourselves by movement. Movement for us has become a way of life. We travel for pleasure, in our own country, in foreign lands. Few people are more inveterate tourists.

For us our land frontiers are now things of the past, but we are constantly finding new frontiers of knowledge, new areas for exploration, new worlds to conquer. Much is heard today of the space age. Men peer into the skies; a few even plan journeys to the moon or to more distant astral bodies. If we no longer expect to find gold in the California hills or a landowner's paradise on the Western plains, we are still on the move, still hopeful, still searching. Perhaps somewhere we shall discover the Happy Isles that lured the men of antiquity.

247

Suggested Readings

The literature on the West is voluminous and growing. Hardly a day goes by that some publisher does not announce another book on the West or on some aspect of the development of the American frontier. The literature on the California gold rush alone would fill a sizable library. An enormous literature on the Mormons, much of it controversial, also exists. Original narratives and later accounts of the exploration of the North American continent make up a vast literature.

Most large libraries possess the monumental collection of travel literature edited by Reuben G. Thwaites, *Early Western Travels, 1748–1846* (Cleveland, 1904–6). A newer collection, *March of America Facsimile Series*, in 100 volumes, has been issued by University Microfilms (Ann Arbor, Mich., 1966). This series provides photographic reproductions of many early narratives describing the exploration and settlement of the West.

The reading list below is necessarily condensed and can give only a few of the many valuable works in the field. In some of the most important and more recent works, bibliographies will be found to supplement the brief list included here. In several instances, volumes containing significant bibliographies are noted and recommended.

Abernethy, Thomas P., *Three Virginia Frontiers*. Baton Rouge, La., 1940 .

———, *Western Lands and the American Revolution*. New York, 1937.

Alden, John R., *Pioneer America*. New York, 1966. Contains a brief but up-to-date bibliography.

Alvord, Clarence W., and Bidgood, Lee, *The First Explorations of the Trans-Allegheny Region by the Virginians, 1650–1674*. Cleveland, 1912.

Ames, Seth, ed., *The Works of Fisher Ames*. Boston, 1854.

Athearn, Robert G., *William Tecumseh Sherman and the Settlement of the West*. Norman, Okla., 1956.

Bakeless, John, *Daniel Boone*. New York, 1939.

———, *The Eyes of Discovery*. Philadelphia, 1950.

———, *Lewis and Clark, Partners in Discovery*. New York, 1947.

Billington, Ray A., *The Far Western Frontier, 1830–1860*. New York, 1949; reprinted 1956. Useful bibliographical essay.

———, ed., *Soldier and Brave. Indian and Military Affairs in the Trans-Mississippi West, Including a Guide to Historic Sites and Landmarks*. Vol. XII, The National Survey of Historic Sites and Buildings. National Park Service. New York, 1963 .

———, and Hedges, J. B., *Westward Expansion*. New York, 1949; 3d ed., 1967. Full biographical information.

Bode, Carl, ed., *American Life in the 1840's*. New York, 1967.

Brandon, William, *The American Heritage Book of Indians*. New York, 1961.

Chittenden, Hiram M., *The American Fur Trade of the Far West*. 3 vols., New York, 1902; reprinted 1935.

Cleland, Robert G., *A History of California: The American Period*. New York, 1922; often reprinted.

———, *This Reckless Breed of Men*. New York, 1950.

Clemens, Samuel (Mark Twain), *Life on the Mississippi*. Boston, 1883; reprinted many times since.

———, *Roughing It*. Hartford, Conn., 1872; reprinted many times since.

Cotterill, Robert S., *History of Pioneer Kentucky*. Cincinnati, 1917.

Dale, Edward Everett, *Cow Country*. Norman, Okla., 1942.

————, *The Range Cattle Industry*. Norman, Okla., 1930.

De Voto, Bernard, *Across the Wide Missouri*. Boston, 1947.

————, ed., *The Journals of Lewis and Clark,* Boston, 1953.

————, *Mark Twain's America*. Boston, 1932.

————, *The Year of Decision, 1846*. Boston, 1943.

Dick, Everett N., *The Sod-House Frontier, 1854–1890*. New York, 1937.

————, *Vanguards of the Frontier*. New York, 1941.

Dobie, J. Frank, *Guide to Life and Literature of the Southwest*. Dallas, Texas, 1943; revised ed., 1952. Gives short shrift to some of the phonies who write about cowboys and the West.

————, *The Longhorns*. Boston, 1941.

Esarey, Logan, *The Indiana Home*. Crawfordsville, Ind., 1943.

Ferris, Robert G., ed., *Prospector, Cowhand, and Sodbuster: Historic Places Associated with the Mining, Ranching, and Farming Frontiers in the Trans-Mississippi West*. Vol. XI, The National Survey of Historic Sites and Buildings. National Park Service, Washington, D.C., 1967.

Fite, Gilbert, *The Farmer's Frontier, 1865–1900*. New York, 1966.

Frantz, Joe B., and Choate, Julian E., *The American Cowboy: The Myth and the Reality*. Norman, Okla., 1955.

Gates, Paul W., *Agriculture and the Civil War*. New York, 1965.

————, *Fifty Million Acres: Conflicts over Kansas Land Policy, 1854–90*. Ithaca, N.Y., 1954.

Gregg, Josiah, *Commerce of the Prairies*. 2 vols., New York, 1844; reissued Norman, Okla., 1954 and frequently elsewhere.

Hafen, Leroy R., and Young, Francis M., *Fort Laramie and the Pageant of the West, 1834–1890*. Glendale, Calif., 1938.

Hawgood, John A., *America's Western Frontiers*. New York, 1967. Has a useful and up-to-date bibliography.

Holbrook, Stewart H., *The Story of American Railroads*. New York, 1947.

Hosmer, James K., *The History of the Louisiana Purchase*, New York, 1902.

Josephy, Alvin M., Jr., *The Nez Perce Indians and the Opening of the Northwest*. New Haven, 1965.

Lavender, David, *The American Heritage History of the Great West*. New York, 1965.

———, *Bent's Fort*. New York, 1954.

Lewis, Oscar, *The Big Four: The Story of Huntington, Stanford, Hopkins, and Crocker, and the Building of the Central Pacific*. New York, 1938.

McCallum, F. T. and H. D., *The Wire That Fenced the Plains*. Norman, Okla., 1965.

Morgan, Dale L., *Jedediah Smith and the Opening of the West*. Indianapolis, 1953; reissued Lincoln, Nebr., 1964.

Paul, Rodman W., *California Gold: The Beginning of Mining in the Far West*. Cambridge, Mass., 1947.

———, *Mining Frontiers of the Far West, 1848–1880*. New York, 1963. Has valuable bibliography.

Pelzer, Louis, *The Cattlemen's Frontier*. Glendale, Calif., 1936.

Royce, Sarah, *A Frontier Lady: Recollections of the Gold Rush and Early California*, Ralph H. Gabriel, ed. New Haven, 1932.

Stegner, Wallace E., *The Gathering of Zion: The Story of the Mormon Trail*. New York, 1964. Has comment on the controversial nature of Mormon bibliography.

Stewart, George R., *The California Trail*. New York, 1962.

Thwaites, Reuben G., ed., *The Original Journals of the Lewis and Clark Expedition*. 8 vols., New York, 1904–5.

Tilden, Freeman, *Following the Frontier with F. Jay Haynes, Pioneer Photographer of the Old West*. New York, 1964.

Toulmin, Harry, *The Western Country in 1793: Reports on Kentucky and Virginia*, Marion Tinling and Godfrey Davies, eds. San Marino, Calif., 1948.

Towne, Charles W., and Wentworth, Edward N., *Cattle and Men*. Norman, Okla., 1955.

Turner, Frederick Jackson, *The Frontier in American History*. New York, 1920.

Twain, Mark. *See* Clemens, Samuel.

Vandiveer, Clarence A., *The Fur-Trade and Early Western Exploration*. Cleveland, 1929.

Webb, Walter P., *The Great Frontier*. Boston, 1952.

———, *The Great Plains*. Boston, 1931.

West, Ray B., *Kingdom of the Saints: The Story of Brigham Young and the Mormons*. New York, 1957.

Winther, Oscar O., *The Great Northwest: A History*. New York, 1947.

———, *The Transportation Frontier: Trans-Mississippi West, 1865–1890*. New York, 1964. Has valuable bibliography.

———, *Via Western Express and Stagecoach*. Stanford, Calif., 1945.

Wright, Louis B., *The Atlantic Frontier*. New York, 1947; reissued Ithaca, N.Y., 1959, 1963.

———, *Culture on the Moving Frontier*. Bloomington, Ind., 1955; reissued New York, 1961.

———, ed., *The Prose Works of William Byrd of Westover*. Cambridge, Mass., 1966.

Young, Kimball, *Isn't One Wife Enough? The Story of Mormon Polygamy*. New York, 1954.

Notes to Chapter 2

1. Clarence W. Alvord and Lee Bidgood, *The First Explorations of the Trans-Allegheny Region by the Virginians, 1650–1674* (Cleveland, 1912), pp. 30–31.
2. Louis B. Wright (ed.), *The Prose Works of William Byrd of Westover* (Cambridge, Mass., 1966), pp. 307–8.
3. Alvord and Bidgood, *op. cit.*, p. 110.

Notes to Chapter 3

1. Harry Toulmin, *The Western Country in 1793: Reports on Kentucky and Virginia*. Marion Tinling and Godfrey Davies, eds. (San Marino, Calif., 1948), pp. 65, 78.

Notes to Chapter 4

1. Seth Ames, ed., *The Works of Fisher Ames* (Boston, 1869), I, pp. 323–34.
2. James K. Hosmer, *The History of the Louisiana Purchase* (New York, 1902), pp. 175–76.

Index

Figures in italics refer to pages on which illustrations occur.

255

256